Serrhium Pr.
Thasos
Thasos
Aenus
Sarpedonium Pr.
Samothrace
Imbros
Sestos
Lampsacus
Athos M.
Ilium
PHRYGIA
Scamander Fl.
Ida M.
Hephaestia
Myrina
Lemnos
Tenedos
Mare Aegaeum
Lectum Pr.
Sin. Adramyttenus
MYSIA
Methymna
Mytilene
Atarneus
Lesbos
Caicus Fl.
Elaea
Arginussae
Scyros
Phocaea
Cyme
Hermus F.
Magnesia
Smyrna Vet.
Cyme
Chios
Erythra
Clazomenae
Teos
Lebedus
Colophon
Notium
Sin. Caystrius
Ephesus
Geraestus Pr.
Andros
Icaria
Samos
Mycale M.
Myus
Priene
Miletus
Lade
Ceos
Myconos
Rhenea
Delos
Myndus
Cyclades
Naxos
Paros
Halicarnassus
Amorgos
Cos
Cnidus
Telus
Therasia
Thera

Modern Echoes from Ancient Hills

Our Greek Heritage

"We do not say that a man who takes no interest in politics minds his own business. We say he has no business here at all."—Pericles

Modern Echoes from Ancient Hills
Our Greek Heritage

By
Marvin J. Bertoch
and
Julia Brixen Bertoch

Edited by
Stan Larson

Blue Ribbon Publications
Salt Lake City

Blue Ribbon Publications is an imprint of Freethinker Press.

∞ *Modern Echoes from Ancient Hills: Our Greek Heritage* was printed on acid-free paper, and meets the permanence of paper requirements of the American National Standard for Information Sciences. This book was composed, printed, and bound in the United States.

The frontispiece of Pericles is reproduced from Arthur J. Grant, *Greece in the Age of Pericles* (1897). The map of Greece on the endsheets a~~nd the map of Athens in the text are~~ is reproduced from Evelyn Abbott, *Pericles and the Golden Age of Athens* (1891).

02 01 00 99 98 6 5 4 3 2 1

Library of Congress Cataloging-in-Publication Data

Bertoch, Marvin J.
Modern echoes from ancient hills : our Greek heritage / by Marvin J. Bertoch and Julia Brixen Bertoch / edited by Stan Larson.
p. cm.
Includes bibliographical references and index.
ISBN 0-9634732-5-5 (alk. paper)
1. Pericles, 499-429 B.C. 2. Aspasia. 3. Athens (Greece)--Civilization. 4. Statesmen--Greece--Athens--Biography. 5. Greece--History--Athenian Supremacy, 479-431 B.C. I. Bertoch, Julia Brixen. II. Larson, Stan. III. Title.
DF228.P4B28 1998
938′.04--dc20 96-43404
CIP

Dedicated
to
the Athenian Statesman
PERICLES
and the
Fifth Century B.C.
Golden Age of Greece

TABLE OF CONTENTS

ILLUSTRATIONS

PREFACE

By Samuel D. Thurman[1]

Many nations are said to have experienced a Golden Age at some period in their history, though Greece in the fifth century B.C. is perhaps most frequently so remembered. Sometimes called the Age of Pericles, the contributions of this century to the world of today are probably unsurpassed in the history of mankind.

Dr. Marvin J. Bertoch and Julia Brixen Bertoch have written a history that combines the intimacy of Athenian lives with the impact of those lives upon subsequent centuries, especially our own. The book paints in vivid colors a picture of Pericles and his contemporaries as human beings and at the same time describes with a discerning pen the greatness of an age which also produced Socrates, Plato, and Protagoras, the philosophers; Democritus and Anaxagoras, the scientists; Sophocles, Aeschylus, Aristophanes, and Euripides, the playwrights; Herodotus and Thucydides, the historians; Phidias, the sculptor; and Hippocrates, the physician, together with many others whose names are recalled as contributors to modern thought.

---

[1]Samuel D. Thurman (1913-1995) was a noted leader in American legal education and author of a widely used legal ethics textbook. He was dean of the University of Utah College of Law from 1962 to 1975.

The authors weave the lives of these individuals into that of their central figure, Pericles, the great Athenian statesman. They emphasize that the genius of such intellectual giants, be it in philosophy, art, literature, or science, prospered through the atmosphere of freedom fostered by Pericles. And although the authors' broad-based study of ancient Greece makes it possible for them to depict in exciting fashion the multi-faceted genius of that time, it is in the fields of law, democratic government, courts, and civil liberties that they make their major contributions to our understanding of the Golden Age of Greece.

Many research visits to Greece fueled the authors' enthusiasm for the classical age. The U.S. constitution, the jury system, and the basic concepts of modern law were founded on principles first conceived and practiced in ancient Greece. Athens invented democracy and with it the concept that government should be a government of laws and not of men. The authors have made the study of Greek history a consuming avocation with special emphasis on the fifth century B.C. and the classical age which overlaps it.

The authors, having spent many months traveling, teaching, and researching in Greece, have written and lectured extensively about the law, politics, and literature of ancient Athens. The authors believe that the fifth century B.C., the Renaissance, and the twentieth century A.D. are the three most fascinating periods in history because of the sudden surge of progress experienced in each of them. The fifth century (spilling over into the fourth century) was an island of intellectuality thrust up out of seas of ignorance that extended for centuries before and after. Why that glow of enlightenment burned so brightly for that brief period is a question that each generation should review and understand so that its extraordinary motivating forces may continually be sought, preserved, and fostered. *Modern Echoes from Ancient Hills* is an exciting contribution to that pursuit.

INTRODUCTION

We have spent many weeks inhabiting the ancient city of Athens' hallowed hills. We have long had an interest in the origins of Western law, art, philosophy, and science—all of which endured turbulent periods of gestation in Greece. Like the conning tower of a battleship, three hills dominated the Athenian ship of state: the Acropolis, the Pynx, and the Hill of Ares. In their shadows, the Agora formed the civic center of the city and the Theatre of Dionysus held a mirror up to the face of the world's first democracy.

Law and politics in this first democracy operating in Athens in the fifth century B.C. were similar to, and just as corrupt as, ours today. Yet, under the democratic system, and perhaps largely because of it, great cultural progress was achieved in that century.

In the first democracy, Senate Investigating Committees and the impeachers and banishers from public office were the town meeting and the courts. Any citizen could make his charges or defend his name on the Hill of Pynx where the assembly met, or the Hill of Ares where the Supreme Court convened, or before a jury of his peers at the agora, or in the Theatre of Dionysus. Charges against public officials were being made almost every day. Even then politicians and men of power faced scandals such as the

Whitewaters and Watergates of our own era.

We wandered the three historic hills that ancient men ascended to erect Western civilization. We set up a quiet command post to occupy the Acropolis periodically through times of sunrise, sunset, and moonglow and through the midday madness of the tourist attacks in seething summer. Lost in a dream of recreation, we strolled the stylobate of the Parthenon, looking upward as the Greeks did, to the column capitals and sculptured pediments of that long-lived Temple to Athena. There the worship of wisdom was enshrined and the foundations of modern sculpture and architecture were enthroned.

We descended from the Acropolis, crossed the street, and scaled a precarious stone stairway to the bald peak of the Areopagus, the Hill of Ares—now known as Mars Hill. We sat on the bare stones smoothed by the buttocks of B.C. judges who constituted earth's first democratic court. We stared at the city below from the spot where man was first judged by his peers. We stood where Paul stood when he proclaimed Christianity to the Greeks who soon adopted it, rationalized it, and sold it to the Western world.

We scrambled off the Areopagus, hiked westward, and illegally climbed the high chain-link fence that encloses the still sacred hill, the Pynx. There man's first legislature conceived bills, labored, and gave birth to statutes.

We jogged down the dirt path to the ancient civic center and marketplace: the agora. There man's first juries sat in judgment, Herodotus read his *History* just penned on papyrus, and Socrates persuaded young men that the unexamined life was not worth living and that the search for truth was the noblest work of man.

We climbed back up to the base of the Acropolis, circled its wall to its southeast corner, and suddenly beheld the aged amphitheatre of Dionysus. There, twenty-five hundred years ago, the "first nighters" came at sunrise to cheer or jeer the immortal Greek tragedies and comedies which are still performed today.

We wrote *Modern Echoes from Ancient Hills* to give our readers a historic background. We are much indebted to the Golden Age of Pericles. The architecture of the Western world reflects the contribution developed during that period. This book does *not* follow in chronological order; there is a focus around important places in Athens—the agora and the Theatre of Dionysus (Part I), the Hill of Ares, or Mars Hill (Part II), the Hill of the Pynx (Part III), and the Acropolis (Part IV). Especially out of chronological order is the account in chapter five of St. Paul's dramatic speech to the Athenians on Mars Hill in the first century A.D. The impact and interest of this episode explain its inclusion here.

We hope if you ever travel to Greece and your guide points out the agora, the hills, the Theatre of Dionysus, and the Parthenon, you will relive the debt we owe to Pericles and the Fifth Century B.C. Take the time; fall in love with the romance of the rocks where man first really began to think. Come—hike the hills with us!

We would like to acknowledge the assistance of Winthrop Lindsay Adams, Carolyn P. Bennion, Peter L. Goss, Patricia Lees, Sharon Russell, and Samuel D. Thurman, who read earlier drafts of the text and offered many valuable suggestions. Also, in order for the reader to capture the spirit of fifth-century Greece, Patricia Larson drew the illustrations for the beginning of each chapter from authentic Attic black-figure vases. Tania Tally drew the map of ancient Athens and the Doric and Ionic orders of Greek Architecture.

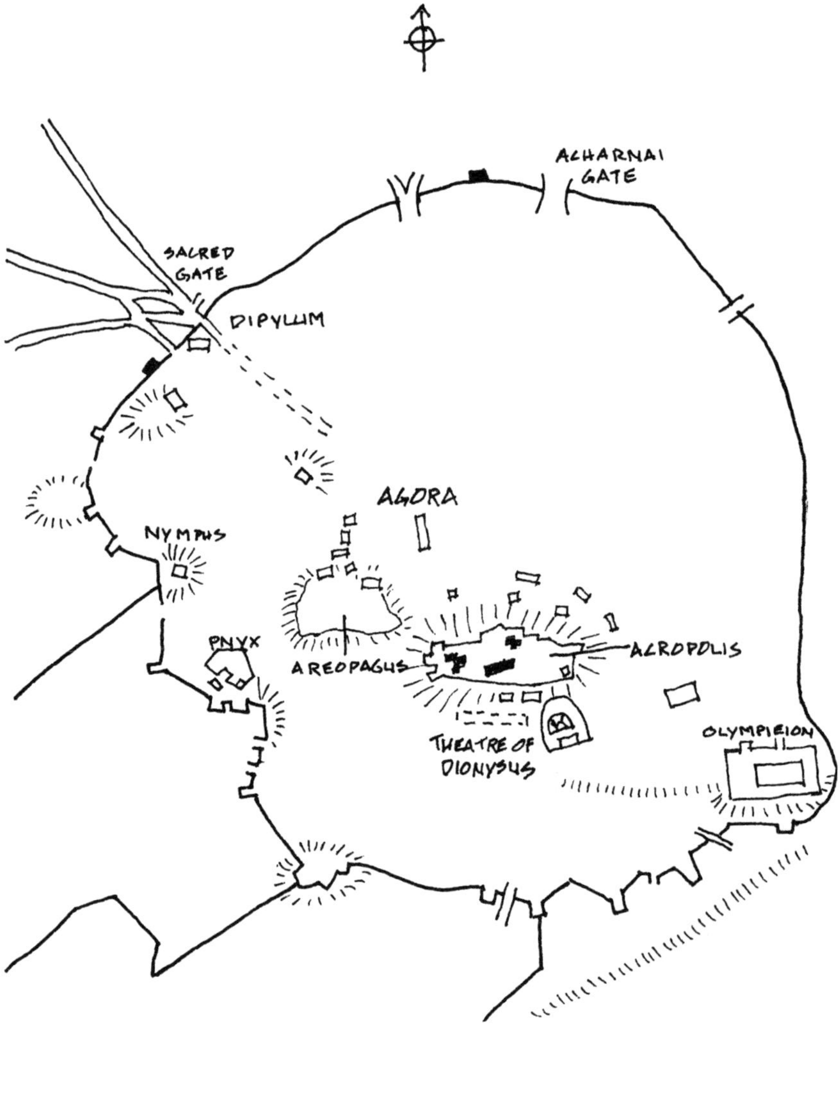

Map of Ancient Athens

THE AGORA AND THEATRE OF DIONYSUS

1

The Heritage of Greek Trials

The Hill of Ares, the Pynx, the Agora,[2] and the Theatre of Dionysus constituted the forums where men, for probably the first time in history, were tried by their peers. Most of the jury trials took place at the agora, which functioned as both the market place and the civic center. English and American jury trials are copied from an ancient institution that found Pericles' mistress (the world's most famous courtesan) innocent and Socrates (the

---

[2]An agora was a market-place, an open space either in the middle of the city or near the harbor, surrounded by various public buildings and temples.

father of philosophy) guilty. Whether criminal justice has improved much over that administered by the first juries is a question lawyers and barristers still ponder. Solon, the Athenian statesman, fathered the democratic jury system about 590 B.C. The first "people's courts" consisted of juries drawn from all parts of the citizenry and set up an oligarchic[3] appellate court known as the Areopagus, or the Council of the Hill of Ares. In 461 B.C., Pericles, at thirty-one, became the Chief General of Athens and a venire of six thousand jurors was established. Athens had a male citizen population of only about forty thousand; thus, nearly one-seventh of the citizenry was called for jury duty every day. The Athenians became a very litigious people. It was great sport and superbly ego-building for the poor shoemaker or blacksmith or silversmith to be able to sue a wealthy land owner and have his claim considered by juries composed of other workers rather than landed aristocrats. Athenians had as much fun cavorting in court as in the palaestra.[4]

The juries handled civil and criminal cases. If you were an Athenian citizen, you could be prosecuted for impiety, striking your neighbor, or seducing his wife. You also could be killed by your neighbor for bedding his wife, and the juries would be constrained by law to acquit your murderer.

On the other hand, you could not be sued by your wife for divorce, if you slept with a hetaera.[5] Divorce laws favored the man. Your wife could not get a divorce without

---

[3]An oligarchy means government by a few and in ancient Greece refers to a city-state in which only a small minority of citizens could be admitted to political power.

[4]A palaestra was a gymnasium or building with central colonnaded courtyard covered with fine sand, where youths in ancient Greece were taught sports (such as wrestling).

[5]A hetaera in ancient Greece was a well-educated, high-class call girl or courtesan, who was also often skilled in flute-playing, singing, dancing, and acrobatics.

your permission. However, if you, the man, wanted a divorce, you simply, without aid of counsel, went down to the tholos,[6] contacted the city clerk, and asked him to make an entry in the records that you and your wife were divorced and that you were given custody of the children. The father got custody as a matter of right, if he wanted it. There was no alimony to pay, but something the Greek men probably considered worse, you had to refund the dowry your wife had brought to the marriage. This deterred divorce because eligible males ordinarily could command a substantial dowry, and to liquidate your assets and return it was often prohibitively onerous. Divorces were relatively rare. Why resort to divorce when you could resort to a hetaera with impunity and retain the dowry?

A multitude of commercial civil suits clogged the courts. A farmer delivered his olives to a shipper's warehouse. They rotted before they were shipped. The shipper refused to pay, and the farmer sued. When did title pass? Who bore the risk? The shipper or the farmer? And so on ad infinitum. Athens in the fifth century B.C. became the leading commercial city of the world. Its renowned and reliable courts became the chief forum for commercial litigation of the entire Mediterranean area. Greeks from Sicily, Italy, Byzantium, Chios, Lesbos, Rhodes, Crete, Corinth, Thessaly, and Macedonia and even barbarians from Egypt, Libya, Sidon, Phoenicia, and Persian Lydia sought the venue of Athens' fair-dealing juries to decide their disputes.

The procedure was primitive but little more so than our present practice. Jury panels were composed of from 500 to 1,500 members. Some writers claim they were from 501 to 1,501, the odd number to prevent ties. Bribery of public

---

[6] A tholos was a round government office building or the town hall, which since it held the sacred fire was also known as the prytaneion.

officials was a common practice in Athena's exemplary city, hence, the battalion-type venires. Not even rich landowners could afford to bribe five hundred jurors. This also explains why six thousand jurors were needed every day. Each jury had its president or foreman but served without a judge. The desirability and functions of a judge to determine the law while the jurors found the facts was not conceived until a hundred years later by the ingenious and encyclopedic Aristotle. In his writings Aristotle set forth the respective responsibilities of judge and jury, almost as definitively as our set jury instructions do today.

Each day the six thousand citizens trooped to the courthouse in the agora and received their pottery chits assigning them to a particular panel. The trials started at sunrise in some corner or other of the agora, in the open air, and each case had to be completed by sunset. Exceptions to one-day trials were allowed if some act of the gods such as a thunderstorm, an earthquake, or an eclipse signaled divine distaste with the proceedings. Postponements, then, continued the trials until the following day. Calendars remained relatively current until the middle of the fifth century, when Athenian justice became so popular that Pericles had to institute pay for jurors, which was previously unheard of, in order to induce enough citizens to report for jury duty.

Citizens on trial in civil and criminal cases represented themselves, even though they could surreptitiously hire a sophist to write a speech for them. Women, noncitizens such as freedmen (released slaves), metics,[7] and slaves had to have someone to speak for them. There was no organized or disorganized bar, no solicitors or barristers as such, but sophists, professional teachers, and writers frequently represented the noncitizens for a fee.

Most of the evidence was presented in the form of

---

[7]A metic was a resident alien with no right to vote.

written or oral arguments. No rules of evidence had yet been devised. Again formal logic, the basis of our rules of evidence, had to wait one hundred years to be invented by the erudite Aristotle. Without evidentiary discipline, irrelevant, immaterial, and incompetent evidence abounded. Parties or their representatives resorted to any outrageous type of irrelevant argument to ennoble one adversary and to defame the other. When the evidence was all in and the arguments exhausted, the jurors did not deliberate. They voted immediately by dropping small bronze discs into one of two urns. The solid disc indicated a vote for the defendant, and the disc with a hole in the center was a vote for the plaintiff. The disc representing the juror's decision was placed in one urn, the discarded one in another. The juror held his fingers over the hub of the disc as he deposited it so no one could tell which disc went into which urn. A majority vote decided the issue. A plaintiff had to receive at least one-fifth of the votes, if he lost; otherwise, he had to pay court costs and some forfeit to the man he sued: praiseworthy practice to discourage ill-considered, nuisance actions.

Writings of the ancients have preserved the drama of some of the more celebrated trials. For centuries the story of the battle of Marathon in 490 B.C., in which ten thousand Athenians slaughtered sixty-four thousand Persians, has been told to school children in the Western world, though our history books sometimes fail to tell the complete story. They know that the brilliant Athenian General Miltiades led the Greeks and that the victory not only saved the Greeks but all of Europe from the domination of Persia. But few know what happened to the heroic Athenian general the following year.

In Athens' dynamic democracy, heroes often soared and sank precipitously. When the eleven Athenian generals, including Miltiades, assembled on Mt. Catriona, overlooking the plain of Marathon, they were awed by the vastness of the Phoenician fleet anchored in the bay and the horde of Persian soldiers spread along the shore.

Miltiades was over fifty, tall, with black hair flecked with grey, flat stomach, and powerful shoulders. He was the stuff of which tyrants were made. For many years he had ruled the Thracian Chersonese as an unchallenged tyrant. To consolidate his power he married the daughter of the king of neighboring Thrace. Even though of high Athenian birth and trained in the republican teachings of Solon, he ruled like a king.

Eventually, Darius sent troops to the Chersonese, and Miltiades had no choice but to bow to him. For many years, he ruled the Chersonese as a client ruler. Darius granted Miltiades much autonomy, and he had fought with Persian troops, knew how they were armed, and what their tactics were. But he hated Darius and the Persians, eventually getting into trouble. When the bulk of the Persian troops built a bridge across the Danube and penetrated deep into Scythia, Miltiades directed his Chersonese to destroy the bridge so that the Persians would be trapped, but his subjects were afraid to do it. Eventually, Darius heard of it and Miltiades had to flee and return perilously to Athens.

At Athens, there were many citizens afraid of him. His reputation as a tyrant was much discussed in the agora and the palaestra; a group indicted him for having been a tyrant. Peisistratus was gone and Cleisthenes had restored the laws of Solon; many feared a tyrant in their midst. However, while at Chersonese, Miltiades had been loyal to Athens. He had captured the islands of Imbros and Lemnos and made them subject to Athens. For that reason, he was found not guilty, and his tribe elected him general of Athens. On Mt. Catriona, that warm, fall day, Miltiades' plan was chosen, and Callimachus was selected to command. The day of battle he dispatched a young man to run to Athens and report.

We recall the youth ran 26.7 miles to the agora, announced the single word "Nikē!" (victory), and dropped dead of exhaustion. Today, there is a race run every four years at the World Olympics called the marathon, with the runners traveling the same 26.7 miles. By late afternoon of the same day, Miltiades also marched 26.7 miles and was hailed as the greatest hero of Athens since the legendary Theseus.

Miltiades' glory was transitory. The next year he addressed his fellow townsmen on the Pynx and sought their support for a conquest he would lead. He asked for seventy ships and the sailors and marines to man them and promised he would bring new glory and wealth to Athens. Some historians say he did not reveal his plans, claiming that it might tip off the enemy and that he was granted his request on faith. Others say he revealed that his object was the capture of the Aegean island of Paros, asserting he was justified because Paros had provided Persia a ship at Marathon to fight against Athens.

In any event, the ships and crews were given to him. He sailed to Paros and besieged its principal city for twenty-six days. He was unable to starve it into submission or scale its walls. The tale is told that he seduced Timo, a slave and a priestess of the Goddess of the Dead, into helping him gain entrance to the city. He arranged to meet her in the sanctuary of Demeter the Lawgiver, in which only women were admitted, but suddenly panicked at the possibility of detection and fled. In his flight, he leaped a fence surrounding the temple and injured his leg. He hobbled back to his ship and returned the fleet to Athens a failure. The campaign had cost Athens a lot of money and embarrassment. His political enemies grasped the opportunity. He was charged with deceiving the people and went on trial before at least 501 of his townsmen.

General Xanthippus chose himself to act as prosecutor. Xanthippus was the leader of a great and rich Athenian family. He had been one of Miltiades' fellow generals at Marathon. He was probably between thirty-five and forty because his youngest son, Pericles (later to have the age named after him), was only three or four years old. Xanthippus, who later led the Athenian fleet to significant victories, was dedicated to his city. At the time of trial, held in an open area of the agora, Miltiades' leg had worsened. He was brought to the hearing on a couch. The prosecutor's job was chiefly one of speaking to the jury and reviewing the evidence for them. Xanthippus may have orated for hours. Miltiades would speak for himself from his couch.

Miltiades, the fallen hero, was convicted, imprisoned for an unknown term, and given the horrendous fine of fifty talents. It is impossible to translate that into dollars today, but it would have been millions. The richest man in Athens, Callias, was only worth two hundred talents. Shortly after the trial, Miltiades died in jail from the leg infection.

The infant democracy had not yet overcome at least one barbarous practice—visiting the sins of the fathers on their sons. The onerous fine could not be paid out of Miltiades' estate. It became a millstone around the neck of his son, Cimon, who was about eighteen at that time. He paid installments on the fine for years and continued to do so even after he had become Athens' leading general fifteen years later. It was only when he married off his sister, Elpinice, to the aging Callias the Rich that he was relieved of the debt.

Cimon must have carried resentment against Xanthippus' son, Pericles, who became his most powerful political enemy. Private feuds often permeated politics and contributed to the volatility of public life in Athens.

Pericles himself became involved in an embarrassing civil suit. His profligate, married son, Xanthippus—named after his grandfather—resented his father for refusing to raise his allowance. Needing more money for wine, women, cockfight gambling, and an expensive wife, he borrowed a substantial sum and signed his father's name to the note. The note matured; Pericles refused to pay it, and the lender sued him, even though he held the office of General.

Our exclusionary rules of evidence today are sometimes much maligned, but they are essential to fair trial and the orderly search for truth, which is the purpose of a trial. Pericles' trial is an example of the abuse that occurs when irrelevant, nonprobative evidence is admitted. Xanthippus, his son, was called by the plaintiff to testify against his father. He had developed a psychotic dislike for his father, and he took this chance to strike at him. He first testified that his father was mentally unbalanced; to demonstrate that, he recounted a conversation, which he had overheard between his father and the Sophist-philosopher-teacher Protagoras. The conversation, actually, is an intriguing example of his father's profound interest in the philosophy of law. A boy had been struck with a javelin thrown by an athlete while the boy was a spectator at the games. The boy's father had sued the city. It was the first case of its type. Pericles queried: "Was the city by any theory responsible or should the case be summarily thrown out of court?" Protagoras and Pericles pondered over the proposition of who was at fault. There was no precedent. Was the boy at fault for standing too close to the playing field? Was the athlete at fault for throwing the javelin erratically? Was the city of Athens at fault for improper conduct of the games? Was the javelin itself at fault? Was it an unavoidable accident with no one at fault? Were all parties involved to some extent responsible?

Hundreds of years before the law of torts developed, here were two enlightened men wrestling with all of its basic principles: fault, no-fault, negligence, contributory negligence, comparative negligence, assumption of risk, and unavoidable accident—all the theories lawyers, judges, and juries encounter every day in modern court proceedings.

Pericles and his guest spent the entire day exploring these concepts and Xanthippus assumed they were crazy. When he observed the jury was not impressed with that diatribe, Xanthippus resorted to a scurrilous charge that Pericles had seduced Xanthippus' wife. The young man apparently not only hated his father but his wife also. The disgusted jury promptly rendered a verdict in favor of Pericles and relieved him of the alleged debt.

Many years later the famous "topless" trial of the hetaera, Phryne, titillated the entire town. Phryne's beauty was the talk of the fourth century. She remained demurely veiled and clothed in public, except at the annual festival of Poseidonia, where, re-enacting the birth of Aphrodite, she disrobed in front of the crowd and walked into the sea. Greeks gathered from all over the Hellas to witness the breathtaking striptease in her finest hour. Phryne was the model of the fourth century's greatest sculptor, Praxiteles. She could command so much money for a boudoir performance that she became rich and offered to pay for the rebuilding of the wall of Thebes, if the Thebans would inscribe her name on it. They refused. Perhaps some influential suitor resented her price and had her charged with impiety. One of her lovers, a celebrated orator named Hypereides, spoke for her, and at a dramatic point he had her stand and then pulled back the front of her tunic, revealing her incomparable bosom. The jurors (men, of course) were seduced. A woman who looked so much like a goddess could not be impious. She was acquitted.

About 438 B.C., Athens was in political turmoil, split on the issue of whether or not to compromise with Sparta or go to war with her. Pericles was opposed to appeasement. His enemies became plentiful and powerful. They were afraid to attack him directly, so they started to work on his closest friends. Phidias, the world's greatest sculptor prior to Michelangelo, had supervised the construction of the Parthenon for Pericles. He and his students had executed the deathless statuary that adorned it, much of which is in the British Museum today. He had created a thirty-six-foot-high statue of Athena in the center of the temple. This superb work of art rivaled the statue of Zeus he had executed in Olympia, which later was immortalized as one of the seven ancient wonders of the world.

The body of the chryselephantine Athena was sculpted of stone, her flesh was of ivory, and her clothes (a warrior's apparel) were fashioned of twenty-five hundred pounds of high-carat gold plates. Just as Greeks today make elegant jewelry of eighteen-carat gold, at that time they dressed a goddess in the purest gold still hard enough to endure.

General Cleon saw a chance to embarrass Pericles by prosecuting his friend, Phidias. Surely, they thought, Phidias had stolen some of the gold for himself. He was arrested and brought to trial at the agora before a jury of the people. In the course of his defense, he requested that the jury convene in the Parthenon at the statue. They did. He put into evidence the city's records showing that twenty-five hundred pounds of gold plates had been purchased by the city for placement on the statue. The plates of gold were lifted one-by-one from the statue and weighed. They weighed exactly twenty-five hundred pounds, and Phidias was acquitted.

But Phidias' accusers were not through with him. He was promptly arrested again and brought before another jury, for Phidias' talented chisel held a touch of levity. He had executed a six-foot-high shield to stand beside Athena, its bottom edge resting on the floor. On its face, he had sculpted a panoramic scene of Greeks fighting the ferocious Amazon women. Relaxed at having nearly completed his masterpiece and possessed of a sense of humor, he included his own face and the face of Pericles inconspicuously among the battling Greeks. Someone eventually observed it, and it served as an excuse to embarrass Pericles by bringing his best friend to trial on the overworked charge of impiety.

It was bitter irony that the man who had most glorified the gods with his works of art, who had given the Greeks the images of Zeus, Athena, and Demeter they carried in their minds, was convicted of impiety and exiled. His lungs lined with marble dust displaced by his own chisel, he grew ill and died in Elis.

The most famous of the Greek trials of the period, of course, is the trial of Socrates, the father of philosophy. Socrates invented the art of cross-examination. He exposed the shallow thinking of many of the high and mighty by tying them in knots with his questions. He embarrassed and made enemies of many of them. He induced the multitude of young men who became his devoted followers to question their own most sacred beliefs and to question their elders. Moreover, two of his most celebrated young students turned out very badly—Alcibiades and Critias. Alcibiades contributed to the destruction of Athens' army and navy by promoting the ill-fated Syracuse expedition in 415 B.C. and then traitorously forsaking Athens to join the Spartans. Critias became the leader of the ignominious Committee of Thirty, which replaced democracy and constituted the government of Athens for a few months at the end of the disastrous Peloponnesian War. The committee executed scores of Athens' leading citizens for political purposes.

Consequently, Socrates became persona non grata with many Athenians, and, in 399 B.C., he was charged with impiety and corruption of the youth. A jury of 501 was assembled, and the prosecutors' arguments attacked him vigorously. Socrates' speech in his own defense, which is one of the great speeches of history, is recorded by Plato in

The Apology.

His fellow Athenians, however, failed to appreciate the brilliance of his speech and Socrates was convicted by a vote of 280 to 220. The procedure for determining the sentence after conviction provided that the prosecution recommend a specified punishment and that the defendant also state what he believed the sentence should be. The jury was required to impose one or the other. The prosecution proposed death by poisoning. Socrates, defiant to the end, proposed an insignificant fine and that he be rewarded like an Olympic victor. If Socrates had proposed something more than a nominal punishment such as a few months imprisonment, the jury may well have saved his life. But they could not assent to his token fine proposition and were constrained to impose the death penalty.

With the capture of Greece by the Romans in 146 B.C., people's courts disappeared from the face of the earth. For two thousand years after the trial of Socrates, the administration of justice was not improved. A study of Sir Walter Raleigh's trial in the fifteenth century A.D. reveals procedure very similar to that practiced in Athens in the fifth century B.C. Gradually, the law of evidence developed and improved the primitive but pioneering procedure of the ancient Athenians.

2

The Trial of Aspasia and Impeachment of Pericles

The tabloid jury trial of the fifth century B.C. was the trial of Aspasia, common-law wife of the Athenian leader, Pericles. But thereby hangs a lengthy tale of love and law. Aspasia was a native of the still-buried Greek city of Miletus, located on what is now the southwest Aegean coast of Turkey. She was the most beautiful and intellectually brilliant woman of the fifth century and must have been among the best in bed. In Miletus, while a girl in her late teens, she became a hetaera, a highly selective courtesan. Perhaps the most literal translation of the word "hetaera" is "female companion." Hetaerae were not prostitutes in the modern sense. Greece had its lower-class prostitutes known as pornae,[8] who charged from one to ten drachmae.[9] But above that stratum of legally licensed sensuality, social psychology of the times gave rise to a significant class known as the hetaerae.

With the exception of Sparta, where women had greater equality socially than in other areas of the Hellas, the woman's place was strictly in the home in the more than Puritan sense. Even in rich Athenian homes, the wife was supposed to be completely absorbed in caring for and teaching the children, supervising the servants, and balancing the household budget. She did not even have the privilege or responsibility of being hostess at her husband's symposia in their home when he entertained the visiting wine buyers or politicians. Those were stag affairs graced only by dancing girls.

Consequently, because the woman did not vote, normally did not teach a child older than six, and had no need to read, she frequently did not have an opportunity to learn to do so. The sexual double standard was severe for wives. Men could philander with impunity, but wives were figuratively locked in. There was, in classic times, little opportunity for a woman to blossom intellectually or socially. Respectable men had far more fun than respectable women.

Presumably, the minds of women were as good as men's then, as they are recognized to be now, and some women, even from the very best families, rebelled against the system and sought and found a state of freedom and

---

[8]A porna (the singular of pornae) was a prostitute or harlot in ancient Greece. Some were slaves kept by their owners in separate lodgings and hired to play and dance at wine-parties; others were kept in the public house of prostitution.

[9]A drachma was a unit of weight and value. There were six obols in one drachma. The Greek silver drachma originally weighed 4.36 g., but later weighed 3.41 g.

equality. They had to have three special talents: brains, beauty, and courage enough to abandon their families and to join the cult of companions long before they attained their majority.

The hetaera was not only a sexual relief source for the man who could afford her, but she also provided the stimulating intellectual companionship that most college-graduate husbands in America demand of their wives today. She had to know something about politics, business, philosophy, and the arts, including especially theatre, literature, music, sculpture, and architecture, which were big in the minds of men of the fifth century B.C. So, the dissatisfied girls that ran away from home and found refuge in the finishing schools known as houses of hetaerae had pretty faces, good figures, good minds, and good ears. Aspasia of Miletus graduated magna cum laude and won the heart and hearth of the great Pericles.

Pericles had been elected Chief General of Athens in 460 B.C. and he was reelected each year (with the exception of one) through 429 B.C. That age of Pericles was the Golden Age of Greece. He was its master of ceremonies. He kept the political climate at a temperature in which the mind of man could grow. The father of philosophy, Socrates; the father of history, Herodotus; the father of medicine, Hippocrates; the fathers of drama, Aeschylus, Sophocles, and Euripides; the fathers of architecture and sculpture, Ictinus and Phidias, were all Pericles' contemporaries whose plants of genius grew in the soil of free expression, which Pericles protected and cultivated.

Aspasia escaped from Miletus to Athens about 450 B.C. to avoid the tyranny of an oligarchic government. She may have come with her fellow citizen Hippodamus, who was Miletus' leading architect, and soon, under Pericles' sponsorship, became the world's first city planner. When Aspasia arrived in Athens, she was between twenty and twenty-two, and Pericles was a vigorous, handsome, famous, and modestly wealthy forty-two.

Pericles had consummated the customary loveless marriage of convenience with a rich cousin about 460 B.C. She was a divorcée. They had two male children, Xanthippus and Paralos. Shortly before or after Pericles met Aspasia in 450 B.C., he divorced his wife. She remarried her first husband, and Pericles, in accordance with his legal right, retained custody of the two boys.

The citizens of Athena's city were no doubt startled, then fascinated, early one spring morning about 450 B.C., as they sat on the wooden benches of the Theatre of Dionysus awaiting the production of Sophocles' new play. The hush which suddenly descended on fourteen thousand theatre goers was not caused by the play's opening strains of a flute but by General Pericles as he entered the theatre and strode to his assigned seat on the front row. Walking regally with their dignified forty-two-year-old leader was an arrestingly beautiful woman with long, golden hair resting on smoothly sculptured shoulders. She was dressed in the most expensive white linen peplos.[10] As the couple took seats, the hush suddenly dissolved into a loud murmur of animated conversation. Who under Helios was this striking female on the arm of the staid and decorous general? No one had seen him with a woman for many months and, annoyingly, the dedicated and discreet general had provided no foundation for even a whisper of gossip.

Now, today, he had suddenly replaced Poseidon as the earthshaker. Men and women craned their necks to examine the stranger. Golden hair was very rare except among the hetaerae who frequently accomplished the beauty crown with the use of dye. But one could easily discern the dye

---

[10]A peplos was a woolen garment worn like a shawl by women of ancient Greece. It was made from a rectangular piece of cloth measuring about 2 x 3 m.

job, by looking closely. Those on the second row, close enough to examine, promptly did so and sent the word up the tiers that her tresses were natural, that her glowing bronze complexion was not the result of makeup, and that her face was the incarnation of Aphrodite.

There were at least four in the audience who would know her: Hippodamus, the Milesian architect and city planner, because she was his fellow citizen, if not a relative; Anaxagoras, Phidias, and Damon, because they were so close to Pericles he would have consulted them about her. As a matter of fact, Anaxagoras and Phidias may have been the first Athenians to meet her. Because of the woman's interest in philosophy and learning of all kinds, she would immediately, on her arrival, have sought out Anaxagoras, the great philosopher and scientist, because he was her fellow Ionian. Because of her beauty, Phidias, the sculptor, would promptly have sought her out to serve him as a model. Hippodamus, no doubt, introduced her to Athens' best people.

How or where Pericles met her is not known. Hippodamus may have taken her directly and presented her to Pericles. He would not have lacked pride in doing so not only because of her beauty but more so because of her brilliantly trained mind. He knew she would be poised and comfortable in the statesman's presence, for she knew the details of his rise to fame and his service as Chief General. She was thoroughly educated on the subject of government; she could quote the Milesian philosophers from Thales to Heraclitus; she had memorized long passages from the plays of Aeschylus and Sophocles and even the young and blasphemous Euripides.

If anyone's poise was ruffled at the meeting, it was Pericles. His mouth must have been slightly ajar for a few seconds as he conversed with this sparkling-eyed goddess, who had the mind of Athena and the face and body of

Aphrodite. Women traditionally carried beauty well, but it was disconcerting to have them converse with the assurance and knowledge of men. Only a few specially talented hetaera could manage that.

Hippodamus may not have revealed to Pericles on their first meeting that Aspasia, then in her early twenties, was an experienced hetaera; that she had been the companion of one or more of the richest and wisest men in Miletus; that men were her business; and that she loved her work. He probably told Pericles at first what was part of the truth, that she was a teacher of rhetoric and politics and that she intended to make her living in Athens by teaching those subjects to boys and to men. That would have startled Pericles much more than being told she was a hetaera. The work of a companion was a proper traditional profession for a beautiful and intelligent woman—but a teacher! A woman teaching men? Or rhetoric? Or politics?

It is likely that Pericles' first reaction to that was negative. He was schooled in the philosophy of Solon who was suspicious of an educated woman and thoroughly opposed to giving her any power in politics. He feared their power of persuasion over men. Men were too vulnerable to their wiles. A lovely new hetaera Athens could use—but a woman teacher? No.

Perhaps it was Phidias, the sculptor, who brought her to Pericles. Sculptors, even the best, were only considered high-class craftsmen, a cut above a cabinetmaker. They made little money, and Phidias' father had been only a poor painter. Certainly Phidias could not have afforded Aspasia alone. He may have hired her with the money the city was paying him to erect a new sanctuary to Aphrodite at the north end of the Hill of Colonus, overlooking the Sacred Way. He was to sculpt a new likeness of the goddess to be known as the Heavenly Aphrodite. She may have been the model because it turned out to be a statue of surpassing beauty. The man who could mold a massive cloud-gathering, thunderbolt-throwing Zeus at Olympia, also could reproduce the bewitching frailty of female loveliness. He had inspired the citizens with the manly Athena Promachos, posted on the Acropolis to guard Athens, but he had stirred their hearts with the rapturous femininity of the Heavenly Aphrodite.

But if he expected his friend Pericles to share Aspasia with him, he made a mistake. There are other credible possibilities. Perhaps Damon, the politician, brought Aspasia to Pericles. Damon and Pericles were writing a new constitution for Miletus. Who could help them so effectively as a mistress of rhetoric and student of politics who knew the idioms, customs, people, and problems of Miletus, her own city? The new constitution of Miletus may have included many of her phrases and ideas. Hippodamus would have recommended her to Damon and Pericles for such a job because Hippodamus, himself an architect and city planner by profession, was a political theorist and governmental philosopher by hobby. He was as excited about writing plans and specifications for an ideal state as he was about designing a building or laying out the physical elements of a city. He would have known of the extraordinary intellectual talents possessed by this remarkable girl and would have wanted someone close to him, planning for the future government of his beloved homeland.

Perhaps Pericles' mentor, Anaxagoras, the philosopher-scientist, brought Aspasia to him, not to help him with his rhetoric or his statesmanship but with his loneliness. If anyone told Pericles this, it would have been the wise and benevolent Anaxagoras: "Pericles, my student, friend, and benefactor, you have had a love affair with Athens for thirty years, but now it's time you had a love affair with a woman. May I present Aspasia of Miletus, daughter of Axiochus."

Even though Athenians were surprised at the new

image the young woman gave Pericles, they were pleased at his taste and the evidence that he, too, was human. The men gazed with awe and admiration and, perhaps, some envy. No one was alarmed until the word spread that Pericles was not returning her at night to a house of her own, in which a hetaera would be expected to dwell, but to his own house, in which for months he had lived only with his children and servants.

When Damon came to Pericles' house to breakfast and work with him, he was startled to see the beauteous Aspasia in the living room with the general. She did not retire to the women's quarters but greeted Damon and joined him and Pericles for the meal. When they left, Pericles kissed her goodbye in Damon's presence and whistled softly as they started down the path toward the strategeion.[11] Even to the unorthodox Damon, such conduct was inexplicable, especially for the august head of the state.

It must have been sometime before Damon worked up the courage to inquire. Pericles' response was straightforward, prompt, and cheery. Aspasia was his wife. Now in his fifties, Damon must have almost spit out what teeth he had left. This woman must have driven his prize pupil and revered leader mad. Because of Pericles' own law, passed at his request not more than two years before, it was impossible for him to marry this brazen siren. She was not an Athenian. The union was illegal. A hetaera kept in suitable seclusion—yes; a mistress, supplied with her own house and estate—all right; but a wife—Pericles was bereft of his brains!

Damon was right; of course Aspasia had driven Pericles mad. Loving Athens was not enough because Athena was and always would be a virgin and intercourse with her was purely spiritual. Aspasia was flesh and flame—the most

---

[11]The strategeion was the office of the generals.

beautiful body and brilliant mind Pericles had ever known. There had been no satisfying sex or intellectual companionship in his marriage. He had thought his work was so fulfilling that he could live without a woman, without love. Love was not a word used often in the average home—a concept not necessarily or even ordinarily associated with marriage. Love was a bed in Corinth or a night in the house of a hetaera. But Pericles had another idea. He had no disposition to lower himself to the level of another man by sharing a woman with him. He had no time to loll at Corinth or shop the houses of the hetaerae to find a suitable companion. He argued there was precedent for his maniacal monogamy. Odysseus and Penelope, Hector and Andramache had had it. So they were of another age. Very well, but what about Solon? The founder of the modern Athenian city-state had advocated love in marriage and castigated the practice of marrying merely for money. If Solon could be a romanticist, so could his spiritual son, Pericles.

Pericles must have exposed himself to a lot of free and fervent advice. Damon was distraught with the possible political repercussions. Over a late glass of wine he must have ranted and raved and finally begged Pericles to reconsider his rash decision. An election was never more than ten prytanies[12] away. What would the voters think of their Chief General taking a mistress into his house—a foreigner—and treating her as a wife. It was an insult to every Athenian woman, and some of them had considerable influence on their husbands' votes. Damon had worked too long, too hard, trained his student too well, devoting his life to the liberal cause. He would not watch it washed down the drain. Could not Pericles see that this romantic madness was for

---

[12]A prytany was one of ten committees of the Athenian Council of Five Hundred, each committee consisting of fifty councillors a presiding a tenth of a year or thirty-six days.

callow youths, not forty-two-year-old generals shouldering, like Atlas, the weight and destiny of an empire? Themistocles was gone. Ephialtes was gone. There was no one left to lead. Cimon, the oligarch, would return from Cyprus a hero and take over the city and democracy would dissolve. The Areopagus would be in the chariot again; the landowners would hog the archonships;[13] the juries would be disbanded; and government by the few would be restored in order to banish government by the many. It would be Peisistratus replacing Solon and relentless history repeating its ugly self so soon.

His friend, Sophocles, would have his say. At forty-five he was the toast of the town. He was molding words into popular plays faster than farmers could trample grapes into wine; and his product intoxicated people more. He could tell Pericles how a man—healthy, handsome, famous, and wealthy as both he and Pericles were—was a fool to tie himself down to one woman. True, an Aspasia with such beauty and brains was rare, but a man would tire of the sameness and the woman would become a shrew—as all women did—from Hera on down.

No doubt, Pericles' sister would have her say. What if a child came? The child would be a bastard and, worse than that, not a citizen of Athens. Suppose it were a boy. When Pericles was no longer powerful in Athens, what would happen to his son, a metic with no right to vote, no right to sit on the Pynx. He could never be an archon, a councilor, a juror, let alone a general—unaccepted in Athenian society, no matter what his father was or had been.

His sister's approach gave him the most pause. A father wanted everything for his son. He must have taken a

---

[13] An archon was an office-holder in Athens. In classical times there were nine, each chosen for one year. After the time of Solon, they were chosen by ballot.

few long walks at night among the pines and plane trees that graced the hill of Colonus, doubtless tortured with that thought. But he had two sons who were citizens. That was enough. They could perpetuate his noble line. Aspasia was knowledgeable. They need not have children.

He did not decide without doubts. He had lived and lusted long for power. Now it was his. Athens belonged to him and he to Athens. Was she worth the gamble? Could he live without glory? Would she leave him with it gone?

But Aspasia wanted Pericles—and she knew her art. As a hetaera in Miletus, she had probably been supported by two or three men at a time. The price a top hetaera could command was too high for one to pay. But, if she could have Pericles, that would be enough. She had come a long way from Miletus. He was handsome, virile, wealthy, powerful, romantic, and amusingly inexperienced in love. He was the king of Athens, and she wanted to be the queen. He was the first citizen of the Greek world. She wanted to be the first lady.

This time there was no reception, no nocturnal parade of relatives from the house of the bride to the house of the groom, no dowry, no eating of the bitter sweet quince, no singing led by a sister, and no ceremony. But, when Damon came to Pericles' house again, she was still there. How in Hades would he sell this to the common man?

At the next election, it was the men who voted, as it had always been. They had seen her at the plays, the panathenaic parade, the review of the fleet, the music contest, and the games at the stadium, always holding onto their leader's arm. They liked her. She was the woman they had all dreamed of possessing. A man had a right to the woman he wanted. They voted for him.

There was only one thing that worried him—she had become pregnant. When the child was born, they named him Pericles. His devotion to Aspasia was the talk of the town. The voice that thundered on the Pynx was gentle and tender at home. He had remained slim, strong, and handsome. He took her wherever he could appropriately take a wife: the civic functions, the theatre, the games, and the religious festivals. He still did not accept invitations to the houses of others, but now he and Aspasia frequently entertained friends or visiting dignitaries. Aspasia, with Pericles' approval, continued her teaching of rhetoric and philosophy and had several students, most of them men as young or younger than she. Some older men also came and some (on separate occasions) brought their hetaera. Aspasia made all who were serious students welcome.

Pericles, junior, was a bright, healthy child and a source of great delight. Pericles was proud enough of this child to give it his own name and refused to ponder yet about the fact that the boy would never become a citizen. That did not matter while he was a child in the home of the Chief General. The tragedy it portended for the future, he would face later. But that cloud shadowed his happiness.

There were five boys in the house now: Xanthippus about fourteen, Paralos about ten, sons by his first wife; and two sons of his cousin, General Cleinias, for whom he acted as a foster father. Cleinias had been killed with General Tolmides in an ill-advised campaign in Boeotai in 448 B.C. Thebes decided to interfere with the hegemony of Athens in other Boeotian cities, marched into two of them, and deposed officials who were friends of Athens. Pericles had considered it a small matter, not worth starting a war. Ambitious General Tolmides appealed to the assembly to send a force to Boeotia to restore Athens' friends to power. He claimed it would be simple, and he could do it with one thousand men. Pericles had vigorously opposed any military action and beseeched the assembly not to dispatch such a small force. He urged them to wait and not to send the expedition at this time. It was one of the few debates he lost on the Pynx. He only spoke on the most important matters now, and he was dejected that the people had ignored his advice.

General Cleinias was elected by the assembly to accompany Tolmides. He probably agreed with Pericles, but he would not turn down an assignment from the assembly. The thousand-man contingent was too small. They were attacked in a ravine at Coronea and Cleinias, Tolmides, and most of the thousand were killed. In earlier years Pericles might have reacted by organizing an army of ten thousand and invading Thebes, but at this time Pericles wanted peace. The building program was just commencing, and he wanted to complete it. If he attacked Thebes, Sparta would probably join the fray, and it would be a bloody, senseless battle. All of Boeotia did not mean that much to Athens. And he had only lived with Aspasia two years, and his son was but a year old. He had won enough glory, and Athens had sufficient empire.

General Cleinias had suffered premonitions before he left and had gained Pericles' promise that, if he were killed, Pericles would raise his two sons. Cleinias' wife had died a few months before. The older boy, Cleinias II, was about eight, and it was already apparent that he was a tragically retarded child. He would never be a credit to the illustrious Cleinias who had been a handsome hero ever since the battle of Artemesium immediately preceding the engagement at Salamis. But Cleinias' five-year-old boy, Alcibiades, was something else. He was the most beautiful child Pericles and Aspasia had ever seen. Even more perfect in features than their own son. Already he was a mischievous, happy, and captivating child, filled with fun and smart as a young Apollo.

One of the most profound sources of sadness in Pericles' life was his oldest boy, Xanthippus, now about fourteen. He was a constant problem. He was completely undisciplined. He would not study. He escaped from his pedagogue frequently, and his bad manners and habits provided grist for the city's gossip mill. Pericles felt the guilt of a father who had neglected his child. When the boy was young, he was too busy to spend time with him. And the divorce had left its mark. Early in the boy's life, his mother Telesippe had not given him the normal amount of attention and affection. He had been raised by nurses and pedagogues, and there was no love in him. Aspasia had tried to break through the boy's negative shield but could not. She had come into his life too late, after the mold had hardened.

His younger son, Paralos, about ten, was more tractable and affectionate to his father but no scholar. Pericles, however, had high hopes and much affection for him.

Pericles could still find little time for the children and, though Aspasia apportioned some time to them each day, she was unwilling to become a slave to them. The independence that had motivated her to leave her family and become a hetaera was still part of her personality. She was opposed to the subservient role played by the Greek wife. She had to satisfy Pericles, of course, and that meant spending hours with their son and that she no doubt enjoyed. That was her security with Pericles. She spent as much time as she could with the general, exposed to the excitement of public affairs. She also continued her teaching, enjoying the stimulation of conversations with many men.

Pericles remained in power and Aspasia became the veritable queen of Athens. Together they endured the bitter political battle that accompanied the construction of the Parthenon. They survived a vicious nine-month war with Samos in 439 B.C. and then for six years they ruled an expanded empire in peace and unchallenged supremacy. Pericles knew that Sparta was going to invade unless he appeased that ignorant, absolutist state with concessions fatal to Athens. He would not concede, and Athens was torn asunder between the party of Pericles and those who advocated peace at any price.

The peace party attempting to defeat Pericles launched a campaign of vilification against Aspasia. The precocious and social foster son, Alcibiades, who got around among the men of the city and had no preference for the democratic system of government, would tell Pericles what was being said at the agora and in the palaestra. There had been a marked increase in the number and prosperity of the hetaerae in the twenty years of Aspasia. The men feared the freedom she taught the women. The women resented the joy her cult provided men. Yes, the "cult" of Aspasia. Some said she had almost as many followers as Demeter, the goddess of agriculture. She was widely loved or hated. Some called her Omphale, the cruel queen who had dominated Heracles, as they say she dominated Pericles. But in Alcibiades' brilliant young mind, if Pericles was not dominated by Aspasia, he was dominated by the disease of democracy. Government by the people then was ignorant hirelings, paid by Nicias and Cleon, walking the streets insidiously attacking Pericles and scurrilously slandering the woman he loved. And Pericles, with armies at his command, permitted it. War with Peloponnesia was inevitable. Athens had to be strong. Pericles foolishly permitted dissidents to weaken it. Alcibiades would point out to his guardian that the assembly was still his, and, before he lost it, he should engineer the banishment of Nicias and Cleon and viperous snakes such as the playwrights Cratinus and Hermippus who used the skene[14] of the Theatre of Dionysus to abuse Pericles, his wife, and his friends. The Chief General was strong and he acted weak. He held a sword in his hand and gestured with a sliver. He should not submit to this malicious calumny

---

[14]A skene was a building forming the architectural background of the stage in a Greek theatre.

which would kill Aspasia with words and his son, Pericles, with the corrosion of his own hatred and bitterness. The general should rule Athens as it should be ruled—as only he could rule it, with a wise, just, and ruthless sword.

Pericles would pace the room as the boy taunted him. How desperately he burned to do exactly what the boy advised. For nearly thirty years, time and again, he had nursed, coddled, coaxed, and cajoled the citizens of Athens into finally acting for their own best good. He had struggled with dull tools—back-breaking, heart-aching ponderous persuasion, when a succinct decree would have saved a debate. For a whole generation Pericles had never rowed the ship of state on smooth waters. He had dragged it across ploughed fields, patiently protecting his people's new-found liberty.

In thirty years, what had he been able to teach the people in Athens? Only that they had the right to disagree with him, to slander him and his woman, and to call his son a bastard. And all this they could do with impunity, because they were shielded by the democracy he had popularized and the freedom of the political system he had solidified.

One morning that spring he sat on the first row at the Theatre of Dionysus in the stone seat reserved for him and was entranced and deeply moved by the performance of Euripides' *Medea*. That Euripides could shake up an audience, and the best thing about it, one could become absorbed in his psychological thrillers and forget politics. In this play, at least, Euripides was not interested in fighting a noble cause. He was interested simply in his volatile characters. He loved a good story and told it dramatically. It was not Prometheus fighting Zeus to free mankind. It was not Antigone challenging the government on behalf of the gods. It was just an ambitious man and his tempestuous wife having a hell of a fight. There were so many men like Jason who would take a woman from the security of her family, exploit the best years of her life, and then abandon her. And there were so many vicious, self-centered women, like Medea, who would, figuratively speaking, kill their own children to satisfy their vanity. He thanked the gods that Aspasia was not a Medea and that he was not a Jason.

Aspasia reluctantly left the theatre after the tragedies had been presented, as was the custom, inasmuch as the comedies to come would be expected to be ribald. In the afternoon, Pericles waited for Cratinus' comedy with apprehension, because he knew it would be a caustic satire probably using him as the butt of some of the alleged jokes. The freedom he had sponsored had become license. He wondered if today he could take it graciously and laugh at himself. The writers of comedy were not as dramatically detached as the cave-dweller Euripides. They had become politicians, and Cratinus opposed Pericles' policies.

It was worse than he had expected. He was the leading character in the play. He endured the jibes and outright slander until one of the characters declaimed:

> To find him a Juno,
> The goddess of lust
> Bore that harlot past shame,
> Aspasia by name.[15]

Pericles felt the blood rise to his face and his fists clench. Some in the audience laughed and some applauded. He stood, and, as the players continued their lines, he walked out briskly, followed by several of his friends. The more they attacked Aspasia, the closer he held her. He became fearful for her safety. She stayed near the house and he threw a cordon of guards around her.

Finally came the weapon that would penetrate all guards—a summons to the people's court. The charge,

---

[15]Plutarch, *The Lives of the Noble Grecians and Romans*, trans. John Dryden, rev. Arthur H. Clough (New York: Modern Library, 1979), 201.

brought by another playwright, Hermippus, was impiety. Before the Scythian police came to take Aspasia to jail to await trial, Pericles went to the office of the thesmothetai,[16] who were in charge of the courts. Never before had the Chief General gone to an archon. The archon had come to him. By putting up a substantial part of his property as security, to assure Aspasia's appearance at trial, he was able to prevent her immediate imprisonment.

Within a day, the entire city knew about it. It would be the most sensational trial in the history of the people's courts. A rumor had spread that Pericles would never permit Aspasia to be tried. He would hire his own private regiment to escort her out of Attica, and he would go with her to Miletus or to Argos, where Themistocles and Damon had gone many years before.

Alcibiades reported the rumor rampant at the palaestra that Pericles would call a meeting of the assembly and have Cleon, Nicias, and Hermippus ostracized and regain the absolute power he had held for over ten years after the banishment of General Thucydides. There were moments when Pericles wished the rumors were true.

Aspasia confined herself to the house and the courtyard. The boys—Paralos, Pericles II, and Alcibiades—suddenly had nothing to do that would take them from the house. They seemed to close ranks around Aspasia. Pericles felt a warm clutch of affection in his throat that Paralos, son of Telesippe, and Alcibiades, son of Cleinias, appeared to be as distraught and protective as Aspasia's own boy.

The flocks of people who used to come, the fashionable fringe that Aspasia tolerated to hold votes for Pericles, were suddenly absent. It was only a month that they had to wait for trial; the house was quiet and the spring air still. Socra-

---

[16]The thesmothetai were the six archons who acted as judges in the courts of Athens.

tes came to visit with her, Pericles, and the boys. He came often because, though he practiced no obeisance to Pericles, he was extremely fond of both Aspasia and Alcibiades. Needless to say, both Aspasia and Pericles had developed great affection for the unorthodox, barefoot philosopher.

For the first time, Pericles saw his Aspasia have to "try" to make conversation, "try" to smile. She retained a regal bearing, but there was fear in her eyes. For the first time, insecurity assailed her normally impenetrable self-confidence. She turned to Pericles' arms for strength, and he tried to give it.

As a noncitizen, Aspasia was entitled to have someone speak for her at the trial. Who would it be? Socrates? No. He was popular only with the young and actively disliked by a large segment of the adult population. The majority of the jurors were middle-aged or elderly. Sophocles? He would perhaps be the most effective, for he was eloquent and popular. But Pericles and he had recently become somewhat estranged. He appeared to be opposed to the prospective war with Sparta. He avoided discussing it with his old friend. He had become more and more absorbed with the recurring theme in his plays: man must humble himself and turn back to the gods or perish. And Pericles, while not flaunting it, remained the agnostic. He had made no gesture to consult Apollo in connection with the threatened war in spite of urging from numerous sources. One could be sure Sparta would send a delegation to Delphi to seek the oracle's advice and court Apollo's favor. Pericles and many of his people had adopted the philosophy of Protagoras: "Man is the measure of all things."[17]

No, Pericles would not ask Sophocles to represent his much-maligned woman. The playwright would not have his

---

[17]Diogenes Laertius, *Protagoras*, Book ix, Section 51: "Πάντων χρημάτων μέτρον ἄνθρωπος."

heart in it. Sophocles was a hypocrite. All his life he had pleasured with the loveliest of companions and had his choice of the best. It was the rich reward his fame and physique had brought him. But it would not be political for the theatre's champion of the gods to champion the queen of the hetaerae.

There was the brilliant young orator, Antiphon, and for a sufficient fee, he would speak for Aspasia; but he was politically ambitious, and she was not now a popular cause. Pericles would not trust him to put his soul into it and present the plea that Aspasia deserved, and had to have, if she was to be saved.

There were, no doubt, those of his friends who ardently urged him to abandon her. She was not his wife, only his mistress. Anything that was harmful to Pericles was harmful to Athens. His leadership, especially at this time, was indispensable to Athens. If he would send her away, it would blunt the spear of the enemy's attack, retrieve hundreds of votes, save Pericles, and save the city from the demagogues whose shortsightedness would eventually sacrifice Athens to the Peloponnese. It was little to ask of a responsible leader, to set aside his personal lust and dedicate himself to his sacred duty to preserve his city. He belonged to Athens, to democracy, to freedom, and to his people. He could not make his life a lie, his city a sepulcher for the sake of a woman. No woman was worth it.

So they wanted him to be a Jason and abandon her as the Argonaut hero had abandoned Medea. For such friends he had nothing but contempt. He would not live without Aspasia. Pericles decided to defend her himself. He would entrust the task to no one else.

The trial drew an overflow crowd. Because the thesmothetai considered it a case of unusual importance, the balls were rattled through the allotment machine, 501 jurors were selected, and the case staged at the Theatre of Dionysus.

At dawn, Pericles and Aspasia left home for the theatre as they had done many times before in their lives, but never for the purpose of acting as the stars of the performance. They rode in an open carriage with a driver, and the street to the theatre was bordered with people who had anticipated their route. Many stood and stared as though assembled to watch the king and the queen ride through the city for the last time. Some had the bad taste to cheer, others the bad taste to jeer, but most were silent, taking no side.

Aspasia, in spite of Sophocles' advice, refused to wear a veil. Pericles agreed with her. She had never worn one. To start now would be an admission that she had been brazen before. For her, it was a time of trial in more than one way. Reaching the age of forty should have been enough for the fates to ask any woman to bear in any one year, even though she had remained beautiful.

As they rounded the west slope of the Acropolis and started east toward the theatre, the standing spectators pressed in closer and became more demonstrative both for and against. The trousered Scythian archers lined the road and held them from the carriage. Perhaps the charge of impiety was valid. She drew as big a crowd to a parade as Athena. They descended from the carriage and walked erectly past the guards into a dressing room under the skene. She checked her appearance in a polished bronze mirror placed there for the star of the play. Many actors had used the room. Masks of many characters adorned the walls. She recognized most of them: Clytemnestra, who was murdered by her son; Antigone, who was murdered by her own hands; and Medea, who murdered her own children. It was a room draped with the trappings of violence and tragedy. She wondered which mask she should wear?

The archon's clerk stepped in and announced the court was ready. She straightened and assumed again the role of the indomitable Aspasia, the first woman to play the Theatre of Dionysus—and without a mask.

They entered onto the floor of the orchestra. Aspasia held his arm, and they stopped at the door for just a second and surveyed the climbing rows of semicircular benches jammed with thousands. The audience extended above the benches onto the slope of the Acropolis.

At the sight of Pericles and Aspasia, the audience took a quick breath; for seconds respiration stopped and funeral silence magnified the sound of their sandals as they stepped forward. He sat her at a table and took a chair beside her at right center of the orchestra. He looked to the left and gave his attention to the accusers, Hermippus, the mordant playwright, and his aides, sitting behind another table on the opposite side. The silence slipped away. Murmuring inundated the hillside, and the recently risen sun slowly topped the surrounding pines.

The archon, sitting on the stage with his clerks, signaled the priest to commence the customary sacrifice. Fear reached up through Pericles' stomach to his chest. He breathed deeply to keep the paralysis from rising farther. He could imagine it reaching his throat and his tongue, thus silencing his voice. He swished his tongue around his teeth trying to keep his nervous mouth from drying up. He was grateful that the cleric read the salacious charge the same way he had read a thousand minor charges of disturbance of the peace, with a muffled, expressionless voice that could not be heard by half the jurors, let alone the tiers of spectators.

Aspasia listened carefully but appeared unmoved.

Hermippus, playwright, prosecutor, stooge of Cleon, stood and swaggered to a standing lectern on which he placed a bulky scroll. As a writer of comedy, his business was satire, cynicism, criticism, and castigation. His victims included anyone in a position of public responsibility.

Pericles respected his profession. Playwrights could goad generals, archons, or treasurers to more conscientious performance of their duties, if they did not destroy them.

But Hermippus did not prick people to improve them. He sliced people to see them bleed. Pericles loathed him as he loathed Cratinus. They were commercial, dishonest, and ambitious—the prostitutes of politics—and they had attacked those he loved. Hermippus, unlike Sophocles, had a powerful and resonant voice. He performed in his own plays, and the strength of his voice and his ability to act, no doubt, were factors influencing Cleon and Nicias to choose him for this role.

Pericles inhaled a draught of hope when Hermippus commenced. He did not speak extemporaneously, and he had not memorized the speech. He read it from a scroll. He read well, but Pericles knew the difference between reading well and communicating with auditors conversationally, man-to-man. Actors are actors and orators are orators, he thought, and an unseen smile formed inside his lips. It vanished, however, as he listened to the malicious vilification compounded by scurrilous lies.

Hermippus declared that Aspasia had crossed the Aegean to seek her fortune and do the will of enemies of Athens. For twenty years, Aspasia had controlled Pericles with her carnal talents. She had caused Athens to go to war for her city, Miletus, against Athens' greatest colleague, Samos. She had induced Pericles to blockade the ports of the world against Megara. Now she wanted to be queen of all the Hellas, and she had inflamed Pericles with intemperate ambitions to rule the world.

Finally, Hermippus came to the specific charge of impiety. For several years there had been a law that hetaera could not enter a temple; yet Aspasia, fraudulently acting as though she were legally married to the general, had entered and desecrated every temple in Athens.

During most of the recess Pericles and Aspasia said little, with Pericles pacing and pondering his argument. As they prepared to return to the trial, he embraced her. When they emerged onto the stage, laughter and loud talk subsided slowly. The archon nodded, and Pericles stood and advanced to the lectern. He stood there for a few seconds as silence slowly settled on the hill; then he pushed the lectern aside and stepped forward to be closer to the jurymen, where his eyes could communicate with theirs, and he could see the expressions on their faces.

Unfortunately, history does not record what he said. However, since Thucydides made up speeches for Pericles, we present the substance of what he would have said, beginning no doubt quietly with:

> My fellow citizens (his resonant voice reached far up the hillside), nearly twenty years ago I made a mistake. I asked the citizens of Athens to limit citizenship. I asked them to pass a law which would withhold legality from a marriage between an Athenian citizen and citizens of other Greek cities and barbarian lands.
>
> I was one of the first to suffer from my own grievous error. Within months after that bill became law, a beautiful young woman, a citizen of our sister city, Miletus, fled the temporary tyranny of that city to the freedom of Athens. When freedom was restored at her home, she declined the opportunity to return to a legal marriage and sacred citizenship in favor of an illegal marriage to a middle-aged Athenian politician.
>
> She promptly gave that Athenian a sound, intelligent son. As any good Athenian mother, she became his first teacher. After she had taught the boy to read and write and do his sums and obey his father and love poetry and understand democracy, she had to teach him something else much more difficult. She has had to teach him not to cry. She had to teach him not to cry when the chairman of the panathenaic games would not permit his fast legs to compete in the races because he was not a citizen. She had to teach him not to cry when he could not enter a palaestra

> with his half-brother because he was not a citizen. When he turned eighteen, she had to teach him not to weep when his friend was sworn in as an ephebe[18] while he watched, because he was not a citizen. She had to teach him not to cry when he drives his father to a meeting of his tribe and has to wait outside because he cannot belong. She had to teach herself not to cry and not to upbraid an extra-legal-husband, father of her child, who had made a mistake.
>
> But that was but a small part of her responsibilities. She was required to mother and to teach four sons who were not her own, including two who were not even her husband's. Two were sons of her husband by a former wife; two were foster sons, orphaned when their father, General Cleinias, died at Coronea. Those two boys have taxed the talent of the most conscientious Athenian mother, for one, tragically, is without a mind, and the other is a genius. She has cared for the needs of both. My fellow citizens, could you ask more of any Athenian mother?

At least he had their fierce attention. Silence lay on the hillside like a forest in deep snow. He concentrated his communication on the jurymen, while the audience of another fifteen thousand ghoulishly eavesdropped. It was difficult to speak of these torturous personal problems, but he had to mold an image: Aspasia, as the wife next door, to citizens whose concept of her was distorted in varying degrees from porna to queen, from harlot to heavenly Aphrodite, from intellectual snob to salacious siren.

Pericles moved closer to concentrate on another part of the jury. He breathed deeply, raised his voice, and his eyes penetrated into those of his listeners. He did not read a scroll as Hermippus had done—he was reading minds.

> The accuser has said she was not my wife. What do you, my fellow citizens, expect of a wife? You expect first, as I have, faithfulness. Recall, sirs, that the

---

[18]An ephebe was a youth of ancient Greece, especially an Athenian eighteen or nineteen years old in training for full citizenship.

> prosecutor has accused this woman of many things, most of them being accusations of evil influence she has had upon her husband. But in the two hours of the prosecutor's presentation, not once did he accuse her of unfaithfulness to me. She, who, if any, had excuse, because her husband could not fashion a legal bond, is accused of everything but infidelity to that man whose law illegalized her wifehood. The prosecutor accused her of every slanderous charge he could turn his evil mind to, but even he had no grounds whatsoever to accuse her of disloyalty to the man she looked upon as her husband.
>
> For almost twenty years, she has lived with and apparently loved an older man with a longish head and a shortish temper; a man with a heart so cold he is jokingly called an Olympian, and blood so hot he is called by some a warmonger, seeking world domination; a man who is unfavorably known as one who talks a lot and laughs but little. Yet, in two hours of scurrilous, unfounded falsehoods, never once, with all his lies, did he ever accuse her of being unfaithful to that man! Why? Because she has been so faithful, so loyal, so devoted to the man she chose to serve, that even those who would kill her cannot find it in their black hearts to lie about her fidelity!
>
> I say to you, my fellow Athenians, no woman is impious who treats her husband as a god. Yet, this is the manner in which a man as unworthy as I have been treated by this young woman.

He had not practiced persuasion for thirty years for nothing. But never had he asked so much from his art. A lump constricted his throat, and he had to pause and breathe it away.

> Let us as Athenians be honest with each other. The prosecution here seeks not to destroy a woman, a mother, a wife; he, and those who motivate him, seek to destroy a general. They seek to destroy me. And perhaps they are justified in that. *I* don't know. But my fellow citizens, I *do* know that, since our Goddess Athena established on the Hill of Ares the first court of justice in the history of mankind, Athenians have never punished one for the crimes of another. If Pericles is guilty, let *him* be punished, not the woman

> who has humbly served him. If I, Pericles, am a threat to Athens, why does my cowardly accuser attack my wife? Let him have the courage to meet me in combat on the Pynx and ask the assembly to banish me! Do not charge my wife with my mistakes! Don't make her suffer for my sins!
>
> Finally, Athenians, indulge me in this plea. I have spoken to you many times over the last thirty years. I have asked of you many things, but they have been for Athens, not for me. Now I ask you something for myself and for any man who ever loved or loves a woman as Menelaus loved Helen, as Hector loved Andramache, as Odysseus loved Penelope. I ask you to vouchsafe to me a sacred right—not the right to speak, write, read, fight, own land, vote, breathe, see the sunset sky, or worship the Goddess Athena. I ask you to vouchsafe to me the right to have and to hold the woman I love. When all else fades, when sons are grown, and land is bare, and youth is gone, and man, like Odysseus, returns from the world and the wars, he wants a woman waiting. I want Aspasia. Do not take her from me!

He had professionally fought through the pain in his heart, the constriction in his throat, until now. Now, the tears came and he did not turn away from his audience as they washed his cheeks. He swallowed, sniffed, and looked up to the temple on the rock and checked his mind as one would his notes to see if there was something he had forgotten to say. He concluded anything more would dilute the strong wine he had poured. He unashamedly wiped his eyes with his mantle, laid it on his shoulders, stepped back, and replaced the lectern on the spot from which he had moved it. He turned and walked to his chair. He smiled at his tearful woman, sat down, and took her hand in his.

They waited with their son in the dressing room while the jurors filed past the urn and dropped their pottery ballots. Four Scythian guards had joined them to take custody of the prisoner in the event of conviction. Then the archon himself appeared at the door. "Not guilty," he said smiling. The Scythian guards filed out. Aspasia fell into Pericles' arms, and he held her very close.

Pericles, who had been the head of state for thirty years, was again hauled into court in 429 B.C., just three years after Aspasia's trial. In the Athenian democracy the law, indeed, was no respecter of persons. This time it was not a mere civil action for debt, but a criminal charge of misappropriation of the city's funds.

The Peloponnesian War had raged for two summers. The Spartans had razed the countryside of Attica while its civilians crowded inside the protective walls of Athens and its warriors executed effective forays against port cities of the Peloponnesian League with its incomparable navy under Pericles' command.

At the end of the summer's fighting in 430 B.C., Pericles' fleet returned to Athens to find his people strangling in the throes of a horrible plague. The unhygienic condition imposed by jamming the citizenry of all Attica inside the walls to save their lives was now killing them by the thousands.

Pericles' political enemies, Cleon, a crude hide tanner, and Nicias, a rich slave owner, and the majority of the Athenians were crying for peace at any price. But Pericles believed the Spartans' demands meant ultimate surrender and the loss of Athens' empire. At a meeting of the assembly held on the Pynx, Pericles in a remarkable speech gave his people a transfusion of courage and persuaded them to continue fighting.

His enemies, however, were unrelenting. They had the council audit his books for the entire thirty years of his service. They found that in 445 B.C. there was a sum of ten talents, a considerable amount, that was unaccounted for. They used that irregularity to charge him with misappropriation and a panel of fifteen hundred jurors was assembled to try the general for a crime that would drive him from office, if he was found guilty.

Those who could or would remember knew what had

happened to the missing ten talents. In the summer of 445 B.C. a Spartan army of ten thousand invaded Attica and marched toward Athens, intent on attacking the city. Pericles wanted no war at that time. When the invading army camped a few miles out of Athens, Pericles rode out alone to confer with the Spartan king commanding the army. Spartan kings were not wealthy. And with ten talents, a fortune to a Lacedaemonian, Pericles bribed the king to turn his army around and march it back home. When Pericles submitted his expenditures to the council that year, it included this discreet item: "ten talents—for necessary expenditures."

His accounting was approved by the council at that time and the story was spread about the city; the people smiled conspiratorily. Pericles had bought peace for ten talents, and his people loved him.

But constituents forget when they want to. They were exhausted by the plague and weary of war. The issue was not whether Pericles was guilty of embezzlement, it was whether or not his leadership pleased them at the moment. At least the majority of the members of the jury wanted a change. They found him guilty and fined him severely. The assembly then convened, and he was impeached as general and removed from public office after thirty years of enlightened statesmanship.

However, there is a movie-type scenario sequel to his trial and impeachment. Within a few weeks, his successors fouled up the conduct of the war so thoroughly that the people begged Pericles to resume command. At first he demurred. He was tired and bitter, but he agreed to play Atlas and hoist the world onto his shoulders again, provided the people would comply with one extraordinary demand—that they grant Athenian citizenship to his son, Pericles II, born of Aspasia. The assembly met and performed that rare favor, and Pericles II took the oath of citizenship beside his father. Then Pericles resumed power.

THE HILL OF ARES
MARS HILL

3

The Constitutional Conflict

Solon established the supreme, appellate court, which was known as the Council of the Hill of Ares, or the Areopagus, because it convened on the rocky, barren summit of the hill named after the God of War. Of course, the Romans later renamed it Mars Hill, and it retains that name today. A trial is a form of combat and having a court named after the war god is not inappropriate, though courts are man's chief method of avoiding violent settlement of disputes.

The hill is a bare, unattractive, stony eminence precipitously overlooking the agora with the Acropolis towering above it on the east and the Pynx Hill rising beside it on the west. An illustrious legend, dramatized by the playwright Aeschylus in *The Oresteia Trilogy* or *House of Atreus* hallowed the high court. According to the story Agamemnon, king of Mycenae, returned from the ten-year Trojan campaign only to be done in by his wife, Clytemnestra, and her lover. The principle of "blood purge" required Agamemnon's son, Orestes, to avenge his father by killing his mother. With the aid of his sister, Electra, the deed was done. But conscience in the form of the horrible witch-like Furies plagued Orestes. Hoping to escape them, he fled to Athens. They pursued, and he climbed to the top of the Hill of Ares and knelt and beseeched Athena, the goddess of the Athenians, to save him.

She appeared as the menacing Furies hovered near, and announced that it was time for a new system of justice to be established. Man should be judged by his peers. Accordingly, she convened a court of men to hear the evidence and decide Orestes' fate. So man's first democratic court, a panel of judges or petit jury, convened, and, after due deliberation, rendered a verdict of justifiable homicide. Orestes was freed of the Furies.

By the time Aeschylus codified the divinity of the court in 458 B.C., most Athenians had forgotten that it was really Solon who had established the court rather than Athena. The Areopagus was made up of graduated archons who had been chosen by lot to handle the civil affairs of the government. After the reforms of Cleisthenes in 507 B.C., one archon from each of the ten tribes was selected each year. After a year's faithful service, they were entitled to advance to the high court. Only those who had been archons could graduate to the majestic mountain known as the Hill of Ares. To be an archon was to be a minor deity, but to ascend to a seat on the high court was to approach Olympian godhood.

The father of tragic drama, Aeschylus, was one of the first celebrities to be tried for his life before the austere Areopagus. Sometime after the Battle of Marathon in 490 B.C. and before the castration of the court in 462 B.C., Aeschylus, a fearless rebel, was charged with impiety. He was then the most famous playwright in Greece, but the august judges were no respecters of persons. The Eleusinian mysteries, devoted to the worship of Demeter, the goddess of agriculture, was the strongest religious cult in Athens. Its rituals were sacredly secret, and it was a capital offense to reveal them to the uninitiated. Aeschylus, who was not above attacking Zeus himself in the play *Prometheus*, would not be afraid to unlock the mysteries, if it would help him win the prize at the Dionysian play festival. Observers believed that in one of his plays he had exposed some of the esoteric proceedings. He was arrested and taken up onto the Hill of Ares to face the judges.

While Aeschylus was speaking in his own defense, his brother sensed that the judges were against him and that his conviction was imminent. Suddenly his brother stepped to the playwright's side and jerked back his mantle, revealing Aeschylus' bare chest and the livid scars he had received fighting for Athens at Marathon. He reminded the court of his brother's heroism. It was enough. The court acquitted Aeschylus, who had been as great a soldier as he was a playwright—irrelevant but efficacious evidence.

From 490 B.C., the year of the Battle of Marathon, to 463 B.C., the Areopagus ruled the judicial life of Athens from Mars Hill, where the Apostle Paul later made his famous speech, the first Christian address to Athenians. The archons were aristocrats. Only the upper classes were eligible to run for the office of archon, so only the richer, propertied personalities became judges. The common men, though voting citizens, were not represented on the court. The court became increasingly conservative, the keeper of the status quo, the guardian of the gospel of the gods, the preserver of property rights, and the most revered governmental agency in Athens.

The Areopagus had its own investigators and its own prosecutors. When its investigators without search warrants or its own prosecutors without a code of ethics, brought the evidence to them about a man who had criticized General Cimon's military maneuvers, or the amount of taxes appropriated to the priests of Delphi, or the claim of a tradesman who had allegedly been cheated by a landowner, the judges of the Areopagus made the decision. Then the august court commanded the Scythian police to execute its order—be it imprisonment, death, banishment, atimia,[19] fine, or any one of a number of disciplinary arrows it held in its quiver of punishment. Worse than that, there was a constitutional consideration. The Areopagus could, in effect, declare a law passed by the assembly to be null and void. The voice of the people could be strangled. The people could legislate; the Areopagus could vitiate.

The people's courts, the juries chosen from the masses, were declining in power and prestige. A fighting rebel named Ephialtes, and his able lieutenant, an aristocrat's son turned democrat, the brilliant young Pericles, changed all that.

Ephialtes was a member of the prestigious bouleterion. This Council of Five Hundred was the effective legislature of Athens. It was made up of fifty men elected from each of the ten tribes. The qualifications demanded that its members be thirty years of age or older and that they had to be members of the two upper classes of citizens, the pentecosiomedimnoi and the knights—classes based on property holdings. The councilors were elected annually. They met four times each prytany, that is, every nine days, for a day or two before the assembly met.

The assembly was composed of all the citizens of Athens and, theoretically, was the legislature. It alone could make laws. Though only approximately two thousand citi-

---

[19]Atimia means literally "without honor,"and refers to a public dishonor or disgrace, and usually a deprivation of civic rights or the loss of citizenship.

zens (six or seven percent of the total) customarily showed up for the assembly meetings on the Pynx Hill, unless some special issue was under consideration, it was too unwieldy to be left alone to initiate laws. The council drafted the agenda for the assembly. More than that, it drafted the bills to be considered by it. The initial debates occurred in the council meeting, and once a bill was adopted by that body, its chance of passage was excellent on the hill. Often the assembly merely followed the recommendations passed on to it by the council.

Another vital function of the council was to supervise and audit the books of the vast collection of civil servants chosen by lot. The men handled or supervised the day-to-day business of the government: the management of the port; the collection of taxes; the maintenance of government buildings and the collection of rents from the extensive types of government-owned property leased to private business; the administration of the water supply system; the care of the walls, the parks, the temples, and the statues; the supervision of the Acropolis. They also organized the many city festivals, including the Panathenaea, the Dionysia, the feasts of Demeter, the Lenae in late January (another time when plays were presented), the athletic events at the stadium, and Athens' participation in the contests at Olympia which occurred every four years.

The ten generals, one from each tribe, were the top executive officials of Athens. Next came the nine archons. One archon handled lawsuits concerning family rights, another private suits which involved metics, and another the religious activities. The six remaining archons were judges administering the operation of the courts. The council even audited the collections and expenditures of the archons and the generals. To ride herd on the financial functions of these officials was an almost impossible task for the unpaid members of the council. Most of them were retired farmers or businessmen who did not have to work. But many of them would rather sit under the trees of the agora and talk or drink wine or gamble or engage in athletic events at the palaestra. Much of the onerous labor of the council had to be performed by a few of the most conscientious. One of these was Ephialtes, who was appalled at the dishonesty of many of the public officials in Athens. Some of the archons, not being paid, felt justified in profiting from state business. Most of them were affluent, but the rich grew richer feeding at the public trough. There were numerous opportunities for graft. One of the most thriving public businesses was the house of pornae, or prostitution, at Piraeus. Though Piraeus was a separate city geographically, it was part of the city of Athens as far as its government was concerned. The house of prostitution, established by Solon a hundred years before, was particularly popular with the seamen, merchantmen, and tradesmen from all over the world who crowded the precincts of the prosperous Piraeus. It was not difficult for an unscrupulous archon to demand a secret contribution in kind or cash from the girls he hired to work there. The quality of the product did not compare with that available at the Temple of Aphrodite in Corinth. And the prices were indeed modest compared to the schedule the priestesses could command, but, even so, a great deal of money exchanged hands at the house of prostitution. Some of it stuck to the hands of the archon in charge, to the detriment of the city treasury.

The rash Ephialtes did not start with the customary spectacular methods characteristic of a rebel of his spirit and stature. He did not grab a sword, like Ajax, and run amok among the sacred cows. He grasped a stylus and a small slate board with wax on it and started auditing the accounts of the archons with the ferreting fanaticism of an internal revenue agent. He became the self-appointed legislative investigating committee of the Council of Five Hundred—

the watchdog of the treasury.

The council had to approve the graduation of a retiring archon to the priesthood of the Areopagus. To Ephialtes, the first avenue to the reform of the Areopagus was to screen its new candidates ruthlessly. If he could close the door to some of the dishonest, self-aggrandizing incompetents, he could at least improve its quality, decrease its number, and, most important of all, undermine its image by revealing the feet of clay of some of those who wished to don its robes.

So he started by delving into the books and practices of the archons. He submitted his evidence to the council. There were bribe-takers, kick-back recipients, and plain embezzlers among them, and some of them were denied diplomas and kept off the hill because of the revelations of Ephialtes. There were honest, courageous men among the Council of the Five Hundred who would not approve the practices Ephialtes unearthed, and some aristocratic archons were denied their lifelong ambition to be vested with the Areopagitic mantle and power. Ephialtes gained fame, as Aristides had done, for his integrity. He also won devoted friends and bitter enemies.

His most talented and dedicated friend and assistant was Pericles. In 463 B.C., at twenty-nine years of age, Pericles had begun to make himself heard in the assembly. Still too young to be a member of the Council of Five Hundred, he was not too young to speak with propriety on the Pynx. Periodically, he ascended the rostrum to plead for equality among Athenians, for respect of the juries, for freedom of expression on the part of all citizens, and for integrity among the officials of the government.

He had become the chief lieutenant on Ephialtes' relentless investigating team, and even the older members of the assembly were beginning to register their deference as he took his seat on the wooden benches on the Pynx. They knew a promising political prospect when they saw one. He was disturbed but also flattered after his first speeches by the fact that many of the older men compared him to Peisistratus. Some of them were old enough to remember the tyrant who had replaced Solon and ruled Athens from about 561 to 528 B.C. Retrospection, sufficiently aged, expands the pleasant and diminishes the pains of the past. They recalled that Peisistratus had united Attican villages under Athens, instituted the Panathenaea, started the play contests at the Dionysia, given them their water system, and built the first wall. Most of all they remembered he was strikingly handsome and blessed with a vibrant voice they enjoyed listening to, even when he was destroying many of the individual rights that Solon had given them.

Some of the old men in their long chitons,[20] dragging dust and with grasshopper clips in their white hair, touched his arm, and, meaning to be complimentary, told him that he looked like the handsome Peisistratus. He spoke rapidly as the former ruler did, they said, and his voice had the same pleasing quality and powerful ring. The old men on the upper benches liked him. They could hear what he said without straining. He made their ears young again.

Under the leadership of Ephialtes and Pericles, the citizens met on the green hill known as the Pynx, in what amounted to a constitutional convention and stripped the oligarchic Areopagus of almost all of its jurisdiction. The only significant function reserved for it was the trial of murder cases. Most of the judicial power was transferred to the people's courts.

---

[20]A chiton was a gown or tunic worn by men and women in ancient Greece. It was made of wool or linen, usually with a girdle around it. Its length varied from 1-2 m.

4

Prometheus and Politics

Capturing the Hill of Ares was not accomplished by the politicians alone. A playwright played a part. Aeschylus, in his sixties, was still a rebel, a patriot, and definitely a political poet. Though he achieved his fame as a playwright, he was first, in his own mind, a general and believed in fighting for freedom. His epitaph, written by himself a few years later, proved that he was more proud of his sword than he was of his stylus. This verse was chiseled onto his tombstone erected in Sicily, where he died while on tour with one of his plays.

> Here lies Aeschylus, Euphorion's son,
> Who died in wheat bearing Gila.
> His valor the plains of Marathon can tell,
> And the long-haired Persians, who knew him well.

Ever since Pericles had paid for the production of his play, *The Persians*, in 472 B.C., Aeschylus had watched and remained close to the young politician. The rich young scion of the illustrious Alcmaeonid family was the son of a great father who had fought with Aeschylus at Marathon. The young man was brilliant. He would be a leader in Athenian government, and Aeschylus was interested in government. As a playwright, he had achieved his greatest success writing of vast themes, such as the victory of the Greeks over the Persians. He would write again and again of epochal events. They served his talent well. The greatest events were political. Pericles, whose ambition was to be a general and statesman, would be a part of the maelstrom of momentous events about which Aeschylus would write.

No doubt he and the young Pericles spent many hours together in conversation. Pericles would cultivate him because their interests were mutual and his identification with the renowned playwright and general would lend luster to the young man and promote his ambitions.

Sometime between 465 and 462 B.C. (the exact date is not known), but shortly before the successful attack on the Areopagus, seventeen thousand Athenian playgoers jammed the Theatre of Dionysus and watched the production of a new trilogy by Aeschylus called *Prometheus Bound*, *Prometheus the Firebearer*, and *Prometheus Unbound.* The plays created a sensation. Poseidon, the sea god, was known as the earthshaker, but Aeschylus, on that early spring day, precipitated his own earthquake. The reaction to the shocking, sacrilegious drama was mixed and emotional. Some of the younger and poorer citizens stood and cheered; some of the older, more conservative booed and derided the blasphemy of the audacious, impudent playwright. Some, fearful that by remaining to watch, they had participated in the sacrilege, hurried to their hearths after the play and offered up sacrifices far into the night to appease the wrath of the all-powerful and vengeful Zeus.

To many, it had seemed a shameful, frightening production. The most alarming fact was that half of the audience had reacted with shouts of approval, and—may the gods forgive the judges—it had been awarded the prize! Hundreds in the audience would not be surprised if Zeus sent a plague on all their houses which could be removed only by the punishment of the impious Aeschylus. Even young Sophocles, now in his early thirties, was, no doubt, astonished, while those rash politicians, Ephialtes and Pericles, were praising the poison pen of a man who must have lost his mind.

The fable of Prometheus was not new to Greeks, but never before had the story been presented in a fashion which vigorously castigated and condemned Zeus. The story line, as dramatized by Aeschylus, has been familiar to the people of the Western world for twenty-four hundred years and played and replayed thousands of times before thousands of audiences. Revivals of it are seen every year in cities all over the world, and it still projects some of the same impact it had on the startled Athenians who first viewed it.

Prometheus, the titan god who had helped Zeus ascend to power as the supreme god on Olympus, incurred Zeus' wrath first by creating man. Then, without Zeus' approval, he stole fire from heaven and gave it to man. He continued his willful way by showing man how to grow food and make medicine, taught him the arts and crafts, educated him in many other ways, and then championed his case in spite of the disdain Zeus held against man. Zeus had no use for man and did not expect or want him to survive.

To teach Prometheus subservience, Zeus forced Hephaestus to bind him to a mountain of stone for centuries where he was left to endure the elements. Zeus' messenger, Hermes, advised Prometheus that he would continue to suffer until he repented of his insubordination and bowed down to Zeus. Prometheus was stubborn. He believed he was right; he would not kneel to unjust authority and remained tied to the rock until the climax of the second play when, to the accompaniment of lightning and thunder, storm and earthquake, the rock was rent and Prometheus was cast down into Hades.

In the third play, presented the same day, Prometheus remained in Hades for several thousand years, and finally, when he was returned to the upper world, he was bound to Mt. Caucasus where Zeus' pet eagle chewed on his liver. Heracles happened along, killed the eagle with an arrow, and learned that Prometheus would be released only if someone substituted for him in Hades. Heracles persuaded an ailing centaur to take Prometheus' place below, and Prometheus was released. The rebellious god was restored to Olympus, and his role as prophet and advisor to the gods resumed; thereafter, he was revered by man as the founder and savior of human civilization.

Aeschylus was amazingly bold in his attack on Zeus. Prometheus, as he lies chained to the hard rock of the mountain, converses rebelliously with the chorus:

PROMETHEUS

Almighty Zeus! Stiff-necked and obstinate,
Still he'll fall one day. The match he's planning
Will topple him from power forever. . . .
Let him perch on his throne, hug thunderbolts!
Not even they will save him, shield him
Against disaster, dishonor, a fall
Beyond endurance. His adversary—monstrous,
Unstoppable—will outface his lightning,
Deafen his thunder, smash Poseidon's spear
That shakes the land, stirs up the sea.
Zeus will trip and fall, and in his falling learn
The gulf between ruling and being ruled.

CHORUS

These are wishes, not threats, to hurl at Zeus.

PROMETHEUS

His fate, my wishes. All will be fulfilled.

CHORUS

You say a power will arise and outmatch Zeus?

PROMETHEUS

Will give him grief more than I suffer now.

CHORUS

You dare him with words. You should be afraid.

PROMETHEUS

Of what? An immortal—what have I to fear?

CHORUS

He'll send you sharper grief than death.

PROMETHEUS

He'll not surprise me.

CHORUS

Wiser to bow to fate, accept necessity.

PROMETHEUS

You grovel! Kiss dust at Zeus' feet.
He's less than that dust to me.
He has a little moment of ruling left:
Let him enjoy it! He won't rule heaven long. . . .[21]

Then Hermes, messenger of Zeus, comes to Prometheus and urges him to repent, to bow down to Zeus and warns him that if he does not subjugate himself to the great one his suffering will be multiplied, and he will be thrown into the depths of Hades, into Tartarus where the condemned are assigned to suffer eternally.

Invictus-like, Prometheus replies:

---

[21]Aeschylus, "Prometheus Bound," in *Aeschylus Plays: One*, trans. Frederic Raphael and Kenneth McLeish (London: Methuen Drama, 1991), pp. 138-40, ll. 908-40.

No more words. It's happening.
Earth writhes.
Thunder bellows from the deep.
Fire-tendrils, lightning-flares.
Hurricanes hug dust,
Death-dervish-dance.
Wind leaps on wind,
Howling, tearing.
Sky drinks sea.
Zeus did this. His storm.
Themis, mother!
Sky-wheel that turns the stars!
See how unjust my suffering.[22]

Perceptive modern translators of Aeschylus and literary critics are eloquent on the subject of Aeschylus' timeliness today. But they rarely comment on how timely Prometheus was in Athens during the years 465-462 B.C., when this play was written. Aeschylus was not thinking of the ages. His mind was not encased in some eternalistic vacuum. He was thinking of the burning issues seething in Athens at the time he wrote. He did not realize that writers would interpret his work twenty-four hundred years later and adapt his philosophy to the twentieth century A.D., as valid as such adaptation may be. One can wed Aeschylus to the ages, but one cannot divorce him from his own hour. He loved Athens. He was concerned with the problems of the people of Athens in the 460s B.C. And he understood them as well or better than any man then living. He wrote so well for the moment that his words became immortal. But we must examine his words in the context of the moment in which they were written.

Aeschylus' characterizations are clear. Prometheus is the hero; Zeus is the villain. His symbolism is eloquently simple: Prometheus represents man struggling to break the chains of tyranny; Zeus represents the forces against which

---

[22]Ibid., p. 144, ll. 1080-1092.

he fights: unjust gods, kings, despots, the Areopagus! Aeschylus, the poet-general-statesman, was keenly aware of the central political battle raging in his city. It was on everyone's mind, everyone's tongue. It was the overriding issue between the two political parties. Either the Areopagus or the assembly would rule. Aeschylus was on the side of the people. He took a bold stand in their behalf. He, personally, had barely escaped the strangling clutches of the Areopagus. It had attempted to throttle his freedom to write. This was his chance to help cripple it.

Hundreds of the playgoers were naive and saw it only literally—an attack against father Zeus himself. But the more sophisticated understood and passed the word. The great Aeschylus had sounded a call to arms. The common man must have the courage to take up the battle against the tyranny of oligarchs who would set themselves up as gods to rule them ruthlessly. And the play promised ultimate triumph to those who refused to bow and who persevered bravely to the end.

Had the words been penned by the young Euripides who was to become the rebel playwright of the next generation, they would have been ignored as the rantings of an intemperate delinquent; but one could not ignore the wisdom of the aging hero whose judgment had been tempered by time and his loyalty to Athens and its people forged in the fire of many wars. He sounded an alarm which demanded attention. His words were not the ravings of an ardent youth but the counseling of a revered sage. They shocked phlegmatic minds into serious thinking—to awareness of the threat to their liberties.

There is no doubt that, when Ephialtes and Pericles launched their attack on the Areopagus in 462 B.C., the message of Aeschylus was in the minds of many. Ephialtes and Pericles appealed to the fire which Prometheus had instilled in man and it gave citizens the courage to defrock the court and circumscribe its powers.

One can imagine Aeschylus, Ephialtes, and Pericles sitting in a palaestra, smiling and lifting a glass of wine together in a toast to freedom the evening after the successful battle to humble the high court.

5

St. Paul's Day in Court

A fleeting incident has given the Hill of Ares (Mars Hill) another dimension of enduring fame. A sign posted at the foot of the tortuous stone path leading to the hill's summit recalls the visit of the Apostle Paul about A.D. 50. Leaping forward about five hundred years beyond the age of Pericles, we hear the assiduous missionary before the Areopagus. Christ had been crucified less than twenty years before. The irrepressible Paul was in the early stages of his missionary work which, within three decades, would plant rapidly growing stands of Christianity throughout the ancient world.

Paul was born in Tarsus in what is now Turkey. He was a citizen of Rome, probably by virtue of the fact that when Rome invaded his city it granted citizenship to its free inhabitants. Rome, by this time, had extended its empire over most of the civilized world. Greece had finally succumbed to its complete domination in 146 B.C.

Just before invading Athens with his message of the Great Redeemer, Paul had preached in Thessalonica in the north part of Greece and enjoyed heartening success. In Phillipi and Antioch and elsewhere, the going had been rough. Conversion was a plodding and sometimes precarious process. But many doors opened in Thessalonica. There were pockets of Hebrews in every large city, and Paul normally started at a synagogue where the rabbis readily permitted the earnest evangelist to speak. His vehement eloquence drew crowds. Initially, the rabbis thought he was simply promoting another Hebrew sect. He was a modern-day evangelist, a boon to all religion. It was only when they listened that they learned the cult of Jesus was a new breed. While Paul's prophet had reportedly said that he did not come to destroy the law but to fulfill it, when they heard his teachings from Paul's mouth, it was a new gospel. It was not simply Moses magnified; it was a revolutionary doctrine. When they heard Paul tell the incredible story of the resurrection of this somebody called Jesus, they realized it was either a great hope or a great heresy. A few Hebrews were converted. Most recoiled and fought back. The most receptive listeners were those Greeks who had seen something they liked in the monotheism of the Jews and were hanging around the fringes of Judaism and listening at the doors of the synagogues. From Paul they heard something they liked even better: love, resurrection, and brotherhood.

There was a reason they liked it. Resurrection was not a new doctrine to the practicing pagan. Orpheus, Apollo's adopted mortal son, had been killed—torn limb from limb—and he had been brought back to life and made immortal. Dionysus, son of Zeus' union with a mortal woman, Semele, had been murdered in a violent orgy, and his body had been reassembled and restored to life and elevated to godhood.

Resurrection was a Greek word. They understood it. Paul spoke Greek, as did the majority of the people in the civilized world, and they understood him.

Though he was soon driven out of Thessalonica by doubting Hebrews and annoyed Roman politicians who policed the subject cities for the emperor, he had made many converts and established a nucleus of Christians in that city which would endure and grow. He moved from Thessalonica to Berea in Macedonia, where he had less success, and then he walked across the plains of Thessaly, over the Parnassus mountains, past faded Thebes, and down to the once renowned, now politically impotent and declining city of Athens, languishing under the rule of Rome.

In 48 B.C., when Julius Caesar and Pompey had locked horns for the control of the Roman empire, the luckless Athenians sided with Pompey. When Pompey lost, Caesar stood in the midst of Athens, looked up at the Acropolis and the assembled multitude, and ordered the city saved, shaking his head and commenting: "How many times will the glory of your ancestors save you from your own mistakes."

Athens still held its head high, for it was recognized by Romans as a center of philosophic learning in their empire. The rich of Rome imported Greek professors as slaves to teach their children, and, for their graduate work, they and their sons journeyed to Athens to Plato's Academy or Aristotle's Lyceum—both of which had been educating the upper classes of the Western world for five hundred years.

Even the great Cicero, one-time companion of Julius Caesar, felt unfulfilled until he, after becoming Rome's leading lawyer, philosopher, and writer, went to Athens to complete his studies. Even so, Athens had withered. It did not have teachers of the quality of Socrates, Plato, or Aristotle. Its painting, sculpture, literature, and music had degenerated. Its statesmen were gone. Yet, the intelligensia of the world still gathered in that deteriorating city.

As Paul entered the city, footsore and hungry, and

sauntered toward the public square, he knew the intellectual reputation of the place. But he was a man burning with a message and did not care about the alleged precocity of this pagan metropolis. *He* possessed the truth: *He* possessed all knowledge that was worth possessing. All else was as sounding brass and tinkling cymbals. All minds were miniatures to his, for his was illuminated by the Holy Ghost, and he represented the one and only God. His was the message of faith, hope, and love, and all earthly learning would pale and dissolve in that dazzling light.

It was easy to find an audience in Athens. Paul knew where to go—the agora. For more than five centuries, the Athenians, with their omnivorous intellectual curiosity, had ambled to the agora whenever they had a spare moment to listen to lectures and engage in bellicose bull sessions with friends or strangers. He would find people willing to listen to him there. Arriving at the agora, he looked around at the plethora of statuary—the altar to the twelve gods, statues to the ten eponymous heroes, founders of the ten tribes, statues to Demeter and Dionysus and others. Athens had trained the best sculptors, so it had the most statues. To Paul, they were an abomination. The golden calves of Moses' time had become marble statues of a multitude of gods. Heathens worshiping idols!

He stood in the same square where Herodotus had read his *History* as he wrote it, where Socrates had cross-examined friends and foes, and there he told the story of the life, crucifixion, and resurrection of Jesus. There were students from the academy and the lyceum having a glass of wine and spouting favorite theories to each other. There were shoppers dallying and civil servants wasting time. There were philosophical dilettantes who hung out in Athens like a herd of hippies. There were profound-thinking Stoics and Epicureans. They listened for a time, but they were too sophisticated. The fluent, fiery Greek-speaking foreigner had a lot of charisma, but his story was on the wild side, a childish fantasy. They had heard the story of Orpheus. Perhaps their grandfathers had believed in it, but they had discounted it as a legend of their superstitious ancestors. The Orphic religion had declined.

Serious-thinking Epicureans and Stoics challenged his claims and reported him to the Areopagus. The council of the Hill of Ares was still in existence, still meeting regularly on the same rocky hill. Rome allowed Athens considerable autonomy, so some of its old institutions were still operating. The council had plenty of time on its hands, so it had assumed the responsibility of monitoring new speech-makers who came to town.

Paul was delighted to be able to address the high court of Athens. What a story he would have to tell his followers in Antioch and Jerusalem. As he hiked vigorously up the trail, he glanced, as he had before, at the temples on the city's Acropolis. He did not know their names and cared less, for they were ornaments of the decadent paganism that smothered the souls of the poor Greeks. So much labor was squandered on buildings and statuary to stone gods when there was a living God to worship.

He formed the outline of his speech as he walked. He would have to be diplomatic but firm. How could he reach the perverted, atrophied minds of these children who thought they were so knowledgeable? If he could only move them to tear down their ostentatious structures and silly statuary, destroy their false gods on the hill, and find the one in their hearts, then salvation would be theirs.

Paul apparently described the incident and his speech to Luke, a Greek physician and his fellow missionary, for Luke reports it in his "Acts of the Apostles" (according to the translation of the Revised English Bible), as follows:

> They brought him to the Council of the Areopagus and asked, "May we know what this new doctrine is that you propound? You are introducing ideas that sound strange to us, and we should like to know what they

> mean." Now, all the Athenians and the resident foreigners had time for nothing except talking or hearing about the latest novelty.[23]
>
> Paul stood up before the Council of the Areopagus and began: "Men of Athens, I see that in everything that concerns religion you are uncommonly scrupulous. As I was going round looking at the objects of your worship, I noticed among other things an altar bearing the inscription 'To an Unknown God.' What you worship but do not know—this is what I now proclaim.
>
> "The God who created the world and everything in it, and who is Lord of heaven and earth, does not live in shrines made by human hands. It is not because he lacks anything that he accepts service at our hands, for he is himself the universal giver of life and breath—indeed of everything. He created from one stock every nation of men to inhabit the whole earth's surface. He determined their eras in history and the limits of their territory. They were to seek God in the hope that, groping after him, they might find him; though indeed he is not far from each one of us, for in him we live and move, in him we exist; as some of your own poets have said, 'We are also his offspring.'
>
> "Being God's offspring, then, we ought not to suppose that the deity is like an image in gold or silver or stone, shaped by human craftsmanship and design. God has overlooked the age of ignorance; but now he commands men and women everywhere to repent, because he has fixed the day on which he will have the world judged, by a man whom he has designated; of this he has given assurance to all by raising him from the dead."[24]

The reaction was mixed. Some were charitable, some were indifferent, but many scoffed at him when he talked of the resurrection. The speech, on the whole, was not well-received. But one of the Areopagus took it seriously, was

---

[23]Luke was well aware of the intellectual curiosity of his kinsmen, the Athenians.

[24]Acts 17:19-31, in *The Revised English Bible* (Oxford and Cambridge: Oxford University Press and Cambridge University Press, 1989), 121.

deeply moved, and was later baptized. His name was Dionysius. One's first reaction is that it is amusingly ironic that the first man converted in Athens was named after the god of wine. This god represented characteristics which were the antithesis of the puritan Paul. Dionysus was a god of the extremes of human emotion (love, hate; ecstacy, agony; exultation, depression); of revelry, drama, theatrics; and the god of instinct and intuition as opposed to reason.

Yet, on further meditation, it is not ironic or incongruous at all. Jesus was the god of the heart. Moreover, Paul found it was easier to convert the sinner than the slave of the establishment or the theologians. Also, Dionysius knew about resurrection; it had happened to his namesake.

Paul soon abandoned Athens and accosted the wicked Sodom-and-Gomorrah city of Corinth, where he achieved substantial success and established a strong branch of the church. Paul's modest start in Athens belies what soon happened all over Greece. The Greeks were the first to be converted to Christianity. Very few Hebrews joined the church. While Jesus, Peter, and Paul were Hebrews, it was really the Greeks, not the Hebrews, who gave us Christianity. Matthew, Mark, Luke, and John and all the other writers of the New Testament wrote it in Greek. The population of the Roman Empire at its peak around A.D. 100 is believed to have totaled about seventy million, of whom about forty-five million spoke Greek. Christianity spread on the wings of the Greek language and was spread chiefly by Greeks. All the early bishops of Rome (the first popes) were Greeks and conducted services in that language. Many of the outstanding early church fathers were Greek: Origen, Clement of Alexandria, Basil of Caesarea, Gregory of Nyssa, Polycarp, Athanasius, and others. As Professor John A. Crow expresses it in his fascinating book, *Greece, the Magic Spring*: "They [the Greek Church Fathers] blended Hellenism with Christianity, and transformed a Jewish sect . . . into a dynamic Greco-Roman church."[25] The Greeks took Christianity, Socratized it, Platonized it, Stoicized it, and sold it to the Romans.

When Paul spoke on the Areopagus, he was tilling the right soil, though it responded more slowly than elsewhere in Greece. Paul's blunt approach may have temporarily turned off the Athenians. A foundation had already been laid in Athens and all Greece for the message of Christ. The brotherhood of man, Christ's prime message, had been taught by Socrates and made into a tenet of a viable movement by Zeno, the founder of Stoicism in the third century before Christ. The great Marcus Aurelius, Emperor of Rome, became a dedicated convert to Stoicism long before Christianity took over in Rome. Socrates, Plato, Euripides, and Zeno had ploughed the ground in Athens. Mars Hill is where Paul planted thc seed.

[25]John A. Crow, *Greece: The Magic Spring* (New York: Harper and Row, 1970), 226.

The Theatre of Dionysus at Athens

The Parthenon on the Acropolis at Athens

The City-State of Mycenae

The Inner Propylaea at Eleusis

THE PYNX HILL

6

General Cimon's Trial for Treason

Pynx Hill, covering a sizeable section of the center of Athens and fenced in for commercial and historical reasons, is the bloodiest battleground of ancient democracy. It is the ring where the most significant political wars were fought. It is where the town meetings were held, where the ecclesia or legislature of Athens convened. Regularly once every nine days and on special occasions, the Athenian flag was hoisted on the hill to call its citizens to conference.

Covering several acres, today its chain-link perimeter encloses a grassy, pine-studded eminence scarred by a row of pole-sitting loudspeakers erected to project the French-inspired "Son et Lumière" ("Sound and Light") to tireless tourists. This production relates the tale of the glorious fifth century B.C., the Golden Age of Greece. Lofty words and stirring music rend the soft summer night air and enrapture the globe-trotters who trek by the busload to the hill's base and hike to its summit to sit and stare as lights play on the sacred ruins of the Acropolis a mile away. They listen with awe to the words of Pericles spoken in exalted British dialect at eight o'clock and theatrical French at nine.

The ancient assemblymen stood and shouted twenty-five hundred years ago to hammer out in classical Greek, violent with verbs, the noble or nonsensical or barbarous laws, and conduct cosmic trials that decided the fate of cities and significant citizens. Here generals and statesmen were banished, deprived of their property, or tried for their lives. Here pensions for soldiers and sailors or support and education for their surviving children were instituted. Here workmen's compensation laws were first enacted. Here treaties with foreign states were ratified. Here generals were selected, war declared, and peace decreed. Here money was appropriated to produce plays; pay playwrights; support historians, athletes, artists, and musicians; name streets after painters; and grant or deny or destroy citizenship. Here allied cities were saved or their male citizens put to death and their women and children sold into slavery.

Here was the beating heart of the body of the people. Here the power of the benign or malevolent masses built or destroyed, blessed or burned. Here man exhibited the best and the worst in the volatile cauldron of the first inspiring, erratic, glorious, and sometimes pernicious democracy. Here mankind ascended heights and probed depths unknown before or since until the intellectual, scientific, and sociological explosions of the last two hundred years.

In a sense, the first New-England-type town meeting was held on the Pynx in Athens about 590 B.C. It sprang from economic desperation and the vision and wisdom of one man—Solon, the man whose name has become a synonym for senator.

Athens was first ruled by kings, the most celebrated of whom were Aegeus, after whom the Aegean Sea was named, and Theseus, his bold, bull-fighting son. Kings were succeeded by a few families of rich land owners. For generations they ruled the Athenian city state, squeezing the people in an oligarchic, autocratic vise. The state was largely agricultural and, secondarily, a sea-trading society.

Hard times hit the small farmer and sheep raiser. Dozens of small farmers mortgaged their farms in the fall to one big farmer to borrow money to buy seed. Next harvest they did not make enough to pay off the mortgage. That fall they mortgaged their own bodies for another year's seed. When the harvest failed to discharge the second mortgage, they surrendered their farms and themselves to the big landowners. In other words, they submitted to slavery. The city-state floundered in this degradation of being enslaved.

Athenians were good at almost everything but slavery. Thousands escaped Attica entirely, seriously depleting the working population. Those who remained were poor, unproductive workers, for they had lost the incentive to achieve. The large landowners became as desperate as their slaves. Not enough food was being produced to feed even the rich, let alone the poor.

A town meeting was held. Rich and poor alike cried for leadership. Solon, an educated son of a well-to-do merchant, had distinguished himself as a military commander, a poet, and an orator. He was the most admired man in the city. In desperation, they turned to him and asked him to be king with absolute power. He refused a crown, but for a time accepted the role of dictator. He ordered that all Athenian slaveholders free their Athenian slaves. It was done. He broke up the big farms, to some extent, giving back to farmers their lands which had been foreclosed. He created a new code of laws. One of them required every able-bodied man to work, produce, and account for his production at the end of the year. He established the ecclesia, a legislative assembly composed of all the adult male, native-born Athenians. They were to make the laws and choose the leaders—and democracy was born.

It was a cross, however, between democracy and autocracy, for he set up four classes of citizens based on their property holdings. The leaders had to be chosen from the richest class. But it was a substantial start toward the democracy which Cleisthenes, Ephialtes, and Pericles would later improve.

He established juries chosen from all segments of the society and a supreme court called the Council of the Hill of Ares or the Areopagus. While he roughly divided the functions of government into three departments—executive, legislative, and judicial—they sometimes overlapped. For example, the assembly occasionally assumed judicial impeachment and ostracism functions. Impeachment of generals for treason or corruption was a function exercised by the assembly when it chose to do so.

General Miltiades, the Athenian hero at Marathon, had a son, Cimon, who also became a famous military leader. He enjoyed no victory as significant and celebrated as Marathon, but he stayed honest longer than his father and reaped the reward of a series of less dramatic, but nevertheless important, campaigns.

After General Themistocles' leadership saved Athens by pulverizing the Persians at the battle of Salamis, the victory went to his head, and he lost favor. He had been the liberal leader of the masses—the sailors, fishermen, tradesmen, and laborers. Cimon was the candidate of the conservatives, the wealthier merchants, and larger landowners.

Themistocles' military genius was no longer needed, the city reacted conservatively. Aristides the Just took the reins for a short time; then Cimon took over.

Cimon was somewhat less noble than Plutarch painted him, but he was a capable, fearless general and a swashbuckling politician capable of campaign frauds worthy of a twentieth-century statesman. About 474 B.C., after making the seas safe for Athenian shippers by wiping out the pirates, he consummated a simply superb political trick. At the island of Scyros where he buried the last of a contingent of pirates, he stumbled onto the skeleton of an unusually large man. He knew his history and proved himself to be the world's greatest politico-archaeologist. He returned the bones triumphantly to Athens, displaying them in the parade as the long lost bones of Athens' greatest legendary hero, Theseus. He had them placed in a sacred vault, and, in the minds of the masses, the marrow in Theseus' ancient bones was now transplanted into the bones of Cimon, his modern counterpart.

Cimon won a significant battle against Persia on the banks of the Eurymedon River in what is now southern Turkey in 466 B.C., and the next year invaded Macedonia. That invasion led to his trial for treason.

In 465 B.C., Athens received disturbing information of Persian influence in Thrace. It is possible the Persians were attracted by the gold mines. The assembly, at the suggestion of Cimon, decided to plant a sizeable Athenian colony at Nine Ways, north of the Strymon River, located in southwestern Thrace. There were always poor families happy to be uprooted from their indigence and given ground in some area under Athens' influence where they could get a new start. Athens had established many colonies on the coast from Byzantium west. The residents of Thrace and of the nearby island of Thasos had enjoyed a virtual monopoly of the rich gold mines. The arrival of the Athenian colonists, equipped with, among other things, picks and shovels, aroused hostility. Cimon rowed north with the fleet and several companies of marines, infantry, and cavalry. Thasos, resenting the intrusion, withdrew from the League of Delos and arrayed its navy against Athens. Cimon proceeded to battle their navy, besiege their island, and attempt to starve them into allegiance—the pattern he had executed successfully with the island of Naxos, five years before.

Thrace threatened war, Cimon sent a small army deep into its forests and mountains, and Cimon's army was substantially wiped out. The popular General Leogoras, leader of the expedition, was among those killed. Evil word seeped back to Athens. Cimon had suffered his first military defeat —committed his first strategic faux pas.

The community at Nine Ways also encroached on the hegemony of Macedonia, a Greek state with no understanding of, nor affection for, Athens. The Macedonians, 130 years before Alexander the Great's rule, were still a primitive people. They hunted their game and tilled their soil, and about their only contact with the outside world was their worship of the Oracle at Delphi and their exportation of vast amounts of timber to the less-forested areas of Attica, Thessaly, and Ionia. They glowered at the Athenian colony and mobilized their army, for they had heard how ambitious and aggrandizing Athenians were. Cimon was not about to have his colonists driven out, and war between Athens and Macedonia resulted.

While the battle with Thasos was eventually won, and the island's loyalty to the league forcibly restored, the campaign in Macedonia ended in failure. And as far as the young Pericles and thousands of other Athenian warriors could see, there was no justification for the failure and no reason for it, except the inexplicable decision of Cimon to withdraw and abandon the war when it was almost won. After severe and costly fighting, and with the Macedonians on the run, Cimon suddenly decided to withdraw and return his troops to Athens.

Some of the wounded were, no doubt, transported back on Pericles' ship. As they entered the harbor, some of the suffering dragged themselves to the bulkheads to see the city of their homes.

As miserable as they were, they were stirred by a new sight in Athens which they could behold all the way from the harbor. A goddess with a gleaming spear and shining helmet towered above the Acropolis, as though hanging in midair, an apparition of hope on the high city. It was the giant bronze statue of Athena Promachos (Athena the Protector). Phidias, on commission from Cimon, had completed it while they had been away. Seventy feet high, it was the tallest statue ever created. All on board the returning ship who could move struggled to the rail, stood, cheered, and waved. Slouching soldiers stood straight, and faith for a moment replaced futility.

It lifted the spirits of the returning troops but did not banish the feeling of frustration which the failure at Macedon had given them. Cimon had been the Chief General, the head of the government for more than a dozen years. Until Thrace and Macedonia, all of his military ventures had been glorious victories, but this abortion stirred the ire of his detractors and now his policies on domestic matters were also fair game for attack. Until now, Pericles, Damon, Ephialtes, and others who had been followers of Themistocles had found it futile to criticize the hero. But now it appeared Cimon was not infallible.

There was growing reason for unrest among the lower classes. True, Cimon had bought the friendship of hundreds. With his vast wealth acquired as booty from his battles, he had become one of the richest men in Athens. He built a new wall partway around the Acropolis. He planted trees by the score around the agora, providing pleasant shade for the thousands of shoppers, government workers, and idlers who spent most of their time in the marketplace. He had given alms to hundreds of the poor, and some of them worshiped him. To emphasize how democratic he was, he had opened the gates to his vast estate and allowed all humble citizens who would to come onto his premises and help themselves to the fruit that grew on the trees of his bounteous orchards.

But there were too many poor. He could not patronize them all. There were too many citizens in the arbitrarily delineated third- and fourth-class categories who resented the privileges granted to the upper classes but denied to the lower. They could not hold offices of any honor or significance. They could not run for the office of general. They could not be archons or members of the Council of Five Hundred or one of the Treasurers of the Goddess, who supervised the spending of the taxes of Athens. Young Pericles had seen thousands of them at the Eurymedon and at Macedon, fighting as well and bravely as those more affluent who enjoyed full citizenship. Athens would let them fight as first-class soldiers, but only vote as second-rate citizens. Cimon was the darling of the elite, the well-to-do, and the aristocrats. His conduct at Macedonia brought this heating issue to a boil and made a target of his leadership.

The new leader of the people's party was a hard, conscientious, and fearless iconoclast named Ephialtes. He had Themistocles' rapport with the middle and lower classes, and he was blessed with Aristides' unshakable sense of justice and dedication to honesty. His successful attack on the dictatorial Supreme Court has already been described.

Cimon had been a defender of the rich man's tribunal. Prior to Ephialtes' assault on the court, the liberal party leader had formally charged Cimon with treason and staged his trial, not before the court of the Areopagus, but before the people—the assembly. He asked Pericles to serve on the prosecuting committee and give one of the speeches. The son of the father who had prosecuted Miltiades could not resist taking up the cudgel against Miltiades' son. Pericles believed Cimon was at heart a tyrant, as Miltiades had been in the Chersonese. He believed with Ephialtes and with many of his comrades in the Macedonian campaign that Cimon had made a deal with King Alexander of Macedon—

traded Athenian victory for a personal fortune surreptitiously delivered by the ruler of the backwoods monarchy. That was the suspicion that had ripened or fermented into conviction in the minds of Ephialtes and Pericles. And the recreant voice of Damon, the dissenter, Pericles' political professor, can be imagined, prompting from the wings.

One of the most intriguing features of the conflict between Pericles and Cimon was the role played by a beautiful woman—Elpinice, the sister of Cimon. During her teen years, after the death of her father and mother, she lived at home with her brother until long after the appropriate age for her to marry. She needed a substantial dowry. Cimon, burdened with paying off their father's debt, could not provide one. A young girl's eligibility for marriage was measured more by her dowry than her beauty. Economics was far more important than love. To the upper-class Athenian citizen, love might be found in a bed in Corinth or a hetaera's house on the Hill of Muses, but marriage was a serious sociological and business enterprise. A well-to-do wife was necessary to bolster a man's economic position as well as give him children and manage his home.

The lovely Elpinice, daughter of decaying aristocracy, did not permit convention or unmarriageability to suppress her amorous instincts. While the fair Elpinice and the handsome Cimon lived alone, the tongues of Athens wagged. It was generally believed that Cimon and Elpinice not only lived as brother and sister but as man and wife. Elpinice's deep devotion to her extraordinary brother may have been another factor delaying her marriage.

In the late 470s or the early 460s B.C., the swashbuckling Cimon found a young man on the isle of Naxos who painted with rare talent. He brought him to Athens. Of the many expensive gifts Cimon gave Athens, including walls for the Acropolis and trees for the agora, the painter, Polygnotus, was the most valuable. Cnidus promptly commissioned him to paint a vast mural on the wall at its social club in Delphi. It was a scene laid at the close of the Trojan War and depicted several Trojan women standing outside the walls of Troy grouped around the celebrated Helen, wife of Menelaus and lover of Paris. The most attractive of those attending Helen was one Leodocia, beautiful daughter of Troy's King Priam. Several Athenians who visited the club recognized the model as Elpinice. It soon became widely known that Elpinice was Polygnotus' mistress. Her brother had married the lovely Isodice, and Elpinice found solace in the arms of the brilliant artist.

Later, Polygnotus adorned the city of Athens with murals, which became the most famous of the age. The people's favorite was the one on the stoa[26] on the northeast corner of the agora. Because of it, the collection of stores became known throughout Greece as the painted stoa. For the remainder of his life, the city treasury supported Polygnotus, and the adoring citizens named a street after him. Six hundred years later, the world traveler, Pausanius, admired his famous paintings and the beautiful face and figure of Elpinice, which decorated some of them.

A brother as ambitious as Cimon, who had to double as a father, would not have been above using the assets of a beautiful sister to serve his own purposes. If that was his aim, he succeeded. Finally Elpinice did not have to furnish a dowry. Cimon got a dowry out of the man she eventually married—Callias the Rich—so-called because he was the richest man in Athens. Callias acquired the beginnings of his fortune at the battle of Marathon in a manner which was unsavory, even to money-minded Greeks. All the booty the Athenian warriors found in the camp of the defeated Persians was supposed to have been turned over to General Aristides to be held for the benefit of the city. Callias had other ideas.

---

[26]A stoa was an ancient Greek portico, usually walled at the back with a front colonnade parallel to the rear wall, designed to afford a sheltered promenade.

Immediately after the battle, he cornered a Persian officer and demanded to know where the Persian generals had cached the gold they had to carry with them on a campaign. He threatened the disarmed Persian's life. The officer knew and led him to a ditch where a substantial deposit of gold had been hidden. Callias then ran his sword through the Persian, collected the cash, and concealed it from Aristides. It was many months later when Callias suddenly emerged a very rich man and the story was finally revealed. So Callias became known as "rich by the ditch" Callias.

Callias must have been near fifty when he fell in love with Elpinice. He wanted her, dowry or no dowry. He made a deal with Cimon. He paid off Cimon's father's debt to the city and got Elpinice in return. It was somewhat of a shock to Pericles the night before Cimon's trial, when his door knocker sounded and he opened it and found the wife of the richest man in Athens standing there requesting to be invited in. Pericles, twenty-nine and still unmarried, lived alone with his servants in a house on the Hill of Colonus. The hill was a fashionable wooded residential district near the center of the city, immediately west of the agora, and within walking distance of the important areas—the marketplace, the Acropolis, the Hill of Ares, and the Pynx. It was unheard of for a veiled wife of Athens to wander around alone at night and park her carriage in front of a prominent young man's house and enter it alone. Athens was too small a city for that. But Pericles invited her in, and she stayed for some time.

Everything was against any rapport between Pericles and Elpinice. Their fathers had become enemies, their families estranged, her brother contemptuous of the brash young liberal who opposed him on the Pynx. She had been deprived of marriage for years and suffered a sullied reputation confined to her brother's home, denied the chance for a young and attractive husband, because Pericles' father had condemned her father to prison and her family to crushing debt. Yet she could go to Pericles' house at night, as she did more than once, be admitted, and profoundly influence his conduct.

That night she at first begged him not to speak against her brother on the Pynx. He denied her request. Then she appealed to him to be honest, to be fair. Her brother had served Athens faithfully, brilliantly in the field; Athens had given him riches and glory. Why would he take a paltry bribe from the king of a relatively impoverished country? What was the evidence? Purely circumstantial. No one had seen him take money. No one had seen him meet with the king or a king's agent. Simply because he had made the strategic decision to withdraw his men from a country that was not worth wasting a life for, he was accused by the Icarian, Ephialtes, of treason, and Pericles, she charged, for political reasons, was supporting Ephialtes, his party leader. She knew young Pericles' power of persuasion. She had heard him speak. She knew he had Prometheus' power to give fire to men's emotions and move them to rash action. She knew many of the unschooled, careless-minded, volatile citizens who assembled on the Pynx could be inflamed with oratory and motivated to impose unreasonable punishment based on little or no evidence. Her brother's life depended, perhaps, on the degree of persuasion Pericles put into his speech.

Pericles was goaded into making one of the two cruel statements which Plutarch attributed to him. Perhaps it was because she charged him with lack of integrity or selfish ambition; perhaps it was because he had a questioning conscience about the whole thing; perhaps it was because he was nervous knowing he had the ruthless General Callias' wife alone in his house, her carriage outside his door; perhaps because he had loved or coveted Elpinice himself, and she had given herself to the despicable Callias; perhaps it was because, for her brother's sake, she insulted him by offering her body as a bribe, that he made the unkind, history-quoted excerpt of the long conversation: "Elpinice, you are too old for this sort of adventure."

Pericles did not sleep well that night. After she left, he suffered a torturous siege of soul searching. Were they accusing Cimon unjustly? The evidence *was* all circumstantial. Was he responding simply to his own aspirations? He had listened to Ephialtes. He believed honestly that Cimon had betrayed his city, but could he be sure? Doubt dug at him for the first time. Anaxagoras had taught him something of morality, of fairness even to one's enemies. But morality was ill-defined. What is moral? To what extent do ends justify the means? To a member of the new intelligentsia, such as Pericles, so many questions had not been answered. Which scroll does one open in order to read what is right, what is wrong, what is good, or what is bad? To whom does one talk? Can one ask Zeus and expect an answer? One cannot go to the gods, for it is possible that man created the gods, instead of the gods creating man. By what mountain, beside what stream, through what valley does the road to truth lie?

No doubt Elpinice had reminded Pericles of another disturbing personal factor. After being relieved of the responsibility of his sister, Cimon had married Isodice, the daughter of Euryptolemus, Pericles' cousin. History documents the beauty of Isodice, and the deep affection Cimon held for her. This was a rare marriage of love. Finally, Cimon had found his woman and settled down and had children, and his devotion to his wife was as well-known as his devotion to his sister had been. Now Pericles was a part of a plot to convict his relative—by marriage—of treason which could result in his execution. What of Isodice and the children? Had not the family of Xanthippus done enough to the family of Miltiades?

The next morning before sunrise Pericles left his house and hiked up Pynx Hill with Ephialtes. Hundreds were assembling. The word had spread. A bitter struggle of the titans was on—a special show.

As Ephialtes and Pericles entered the open-air arena, most of the eighteen hundred wooden bench seats were already taken and hundreds were sitting on the ground. They sat on a front-row area reserved for the speakers and waited for the assembly to be called to order. A squadron of Scythian officers with bows and arrows and leather kilts appeared and took their places on the left and right of the three-level concrete structure, constituting the stage of the arena. The man serving as president for the day, his clerks, and heralds marched in and sat on the steps of the stage. The president stood and raised his hand for order. The bedlam of conversation subsided. A priest made sacrifice, drank a libation, and the assembly session officially opened.

Suddenly a cheer enveloped the hill and echoed down to the agora. Cimon strode into the arena, smiling and confident. With complete self-assurance and disarming audacity, he walked to the center of the front row to the seat reserved for the Chief General, waving acknowledgment of the cheers and clapping colleagues on their shoulders.

Cimon had hundreds of friends who would always be loyal. Among the poor there were scores who had taken advantage of his personal generosity and been the beneficiaries of the hired companions who always walked by Cimon's side and handed out money or other gifts to those it served Cimon's fancy to favor. There were those who would always cheer Cimon simply because he was a handsome, colorful, and cocksure leader. His dissolute pleasures induced more envy than criticism. He could steal the treasury of Athena off the Acropolis and there were those who would still follow him to Suza and back and give their only horse for him to ride while they walked.

The debate commenced. Ephialtes' speech scathingly attacked Cimon. Other members of the prosecuting committee addressed the citizens. Cimon vigorously and confidently defended himself. Why should he take a bribe when he was already wealthy and had given away thousands of drachmae to the poor every year and torn down the walls around his estate so those who were hungry could enter upon his land and eat at his table? He pointed at the wall he had constructed with money he took from the Persians to shore up the north side of the Acropolis. Why would a man who would give money away so freely risk his honor by accepting a bribe?

Then he explained his reasons for withdrawing the troops from Macedonia. He was not defensive but righteously indignant toward those with limited military experience who would question his wisdom born of a dozen brilliant victories for Athens. He had pulled his forces back from Macedonia because they were spread too thin and wandered too far from their base of supplies. Lives had been lost a few months before in Thrace because General Leogoras had plunged blindly into unknown, unmapped lands. He would not permit the same tragedy to occur in Macedonia. They had not planned to campaign in Macedonia and did not have adequate intelligence concerning its military forces. He conceded they may have marched on and won a glorious victory, or they may have walked into disaster. Cimon had sacrificed glory to save lives. When he concluded, his partisans cheered wildly.

Finally Pericles stepped forward and took from the clerk the wreath of myrtle that speakers on the Pynx were required to wear as a symbol of their speaking the truth. He placed it on his head and began. He spoke without his customary force and animation. Plutarch tells it all in one sentence: "But, when he appeared to impeach him (Cimon), he stood up but once to speak, merely to acquit himself of his commission, and went out of court, having done Cimon the least prejudice of any of his accusers." The pleas of Elpinice had made an impact.

The vote was taken, and Cimon was acquitted. Ephialtes and Pericles had suffered a staggering defeat.

7

Trial by Ostrakon

After Solon established the embryonic democracy, he escaped administering it by taking a ten-year traveling vacation outside the borders of Greece. When he returned, a dictator, Peisistratus had replaced government by the people.

Peisistratus or his sons ruled for about fifty years before the last in line was assassinated by two young men and their girlfriend. Pericles' great uncle, Cleisthenes, was elected leader. He expanded Solon's democracy, and the people loved it so much, they designed a scheme to prevent forever the possibility of another takeover by a tyrant.

The procedure was denominated "ostracism." The assembly, prompted by Cleisthenes, passed a law providing that one meeting of the assembly each year would be devoted to considering the banishment of any man who threatened to become a dictator. The only limitations on the process were that, in order for the vote to be effective, six thousand citizens had to be present to form a quorum, and at least three thousand votes had to be cast in favor of the banishment.

On Ostracism Day, politics waxed cruel on Pynx Hill. There was no paper, and pottery was plentiful, so old pots were smashed, and one piece, an ostrakon,[27] served as a ballot while another was used as a pencil to scratch on the name of the potential dictator. This is not to say that the assembly ostracized someone every year. Actually, a leader got ostracized only when some other leader stirred up the populace sufficiently against his enemy to get an organized movement going to eliminate him. It became an abused means of removing a political opponent from the arena. As so often happens in democracy, an instrument designed to preserve liberty is used by one strong man or group as a tool to marshal the masses against another strong man and his followers.

Athens temporarily lost some of its greatest leaders as a result of the ostrakon. Just as one can not be a great surgeon today without being sued for malpractice, so one could hardly be a great Athenian leader without being exposed to a vote of ostracism. If America had adopted the system, Abraham Lincoln would probably have been banished sometime during his second term. It *was*, however, a better system than assassination.

One of the first generals to succumb was Pericles' distinguished father, Xanthippus. A hero at Marathon in 490 B.C., just five years later he was one of the two most powerful men in Athens. Themistocles, the liberal, also of Marathon fame, gained ascendancy on the Pynx, and in that year engineered the banishment of Xanthippus.

---

[27] An ostrakon ~~was~~ is a shard, or fragment of broken pottery, containing an inscription.

Two years later, Themistocles also smote Aristides the Just with the ostrakon. Aristides was a genuine gentleman in every sense, but he and Themistocles had been enemies ever since they were in their twenties and had competed for the favors of the same girl. During the vote on the hill, one of the citizens who could not write and did not know Aristides by sight approached the general and told him he wanted to vote for Aristides' ostracism but could not spell his name. Aristides, the mild-mannered hero, chuckled, took the man's shard, wrote his name on it, gave it back without identifying himself, and shook his head as the man dropped the ballot into the urn. However, both Xanthippus' and Aristides' sentences were commuted, and they were called back to serve the city in the wars against the Persians in 480 B.C.

Themistocles was the most engaging of all the Greeks. His genius as a statesman and naval commander sank the Persian fleet in the straits of Salamis in 480 B.C. and saved all Europe from domination by Persia. He ironically became the victim of the ostrakon eight years later.

Themistocles was so popular with all of the Greeks that he probably would never have been banished had victory not gone to his head. He was of mixed parentage—the son of an Athenian father and a Thracian prostitute. Never accepted by the upper strata in Athenian society, when he was crowned with unprecedented laurels for his miracle victory, his rollicking nature overflowed. His riotous revelry shook up Athens. When he raced from Piraeus to the Pynx on his chariot with four naked prostitutes pleasuring him on the way, it was too much, even for some of the common people. In 472 B.C. they banished him, then convicted him in absentia on a false charge of treason. Bounty hunters dispatched to Argos to retrieve him were too late. He had escaped to Persia where he charmed Artaxerxes, the son of the man he had whipped, into supporting him in opulence until his death about 460 B.C.

Cimon, leader of the conservatives, had accomplished Themistocles' political demise. Ten years later, it was his turn. Only a few months after Cimon's successful defense of his Macedonian fiasco, another momentous debate raged on Pynx Hill. The flag went up at sunrise one morning in 462 B.C. announcing a special meeting of the assembly. Rumors had spread—there was a Spartan ephor[28] in the city seeking help for his city. It was hard enough for many of the citizens to leave their work for regularly scheduled meetings, but still more difficult to take off on seeing the flag go up unexpectedly. Nevertheless, before the sundial clocked the first hour after sunrise, the benches were filled and hundreds more sat on the grassy ground at the side of the hill.

Many of the citizens, never knowing how long the meeting would take, had brought sacks containing a flask of wine, a piece of bread, a couple of onions, a slice of cheese, and a few olives. The Scythian guards and archons and the president for the day took their places, and the priest began making smoke as he performed his perfunctory ceremony.

When Cimon strode onto the summit, the majority of the citizens stood and applauded. He was accompanied by a husky man with very long hair, styled as Cimon combed his, wearing a rough woolen tunic and the dark-red cloak of a Spartan officer. Cimon had convened the special session to allow a Spartan ephor, Periclidas, to present a plea on behalf of his city. On Cimon's motion, the Spartan was granted the privilege of donning the crown of myrtle and speaking to the assembly.

Pericles and Ephialtes were suspicious and listened like hawks. An ephor in Sparta commanded more power than a general in Athens. He and four other ephors and two kings constituted the government of Sparta. There was a senate of

---

[28]An ephor was one of the five annually elected Spartan magistrates, who functioned as an important counterweight to the two Spartan kings.

thirty men, but the ephors and kings had the final word. Pericles knew it to be one of the most absolute oligarchies in the world—a complete centralization of the powers of government in the hands of seven men.

The man's Doric accent immediately identified him. One had to strain to understand him. He announced that he had come to seek the help of Athens under the provisions of the nearly twenty-year-old treaty which had bound them to fight the Persians together. He described the terrible earthquake of two years before which had destroyed or seriously damaged most of their homes. Hundreds of Spartans had been killed. This was not news. It had been the talk of the Hellas ever since it happened. The ephor explained that the serfs of Lacedaemon, largely Messenians, had grasped that moment of tragedy and confusion to revolt against their Spartan masters. The civil war had raged for two years and help was needed to put down the rebellion. Otherwise, Periclidas warned, the Spartans might be defeated and Athens would lose its stalwart colleague and be faced across the gulf with an enemy instead of an ally.

After the ephor concluded his dignified plea, Cimon stood and forcefully argued the cause of Sparta. He claimed it was Athens' obligation under the old treaty to unite with Sparta against its enemies. More than that, he insisted, as he always had, that the effective defense of the Hellas in the event of war against the Persians rested on Athens' mastery of the sea and Sparta's mastery of the land. He proclaimed that Athens and Sparta together were invincible, but that each, apart, was lame and insecure. Cimon shouted: "We must not suffer Greece to be crippled nor our own beloved city to be robbed of its yokefellow."

Ephialtes was furious and livid at the applause Cimon received. He took the crown of myrtle and ascended the platform. He beseeched his fellow citizens not to be deceived by the words of a man who was prejudiced by his personal affection for Sparta and its ways. He warned that

Sparta was not Athens' ally; it had entered into the treaty twenty years before to protect itself and had then failed to honor the obligations of that treaty. While Athens had provided the bulk of the ships to fight Xerxes' navy, Sparta had promised to send an army north to fight the Persian land forces. They had sent three hundred men who, with seven hundred Thespians, died at Thermopylae and delayed Xerxes' advance about four days. The remainder of their army had remained on Peloponnesus in cowardly fashion, building a wall across the isthmus so they could hide behind it and watch Athens burn. He warned that Athenians would be fools to send men to die in Sparta.

Pericles spoke next with outraged vigor. He could repeat what his father had told him how the fleets of Athens and Aegina alone defeated the Persians and Phoenicians at Salamis, while the Spartans remained aloof from the battle. Then he proceeded to expound his favorite theme. Athens and Sparta could not be companions as long as their philosophies of government were incompatible. A city of freedom could not cohabit with a city of tyranny. A government of the people, represented by the assembly, could not be partners with an oligarchy. If the Athenians went to Sparta to fight the so-called serfs, they would find they were not fighting slaves but fellow Greeks who were struggling against the tyranny of a handful of landed Spartan aristocrats, even as Athenians were now fighting against the growing tyranny of the Areopagus. They would be fighting for the principle of rule by the few against rule by the many. He attacked Cimon's term, calling Sparta a yokefellow and shouted: "A trireme[29] can not be yoked with an ox."

Cimon's hatred for Ephialtes and the upstart Pericles manifested itself in the bulging veins crossing his temples and lining his throat, as he slapped the crown of myrtle on

---

[29]A trireme was an ancient Greek galley having three banks of oars.

his head, shook his clenched fist in the air, and roared his rebuttal. The noble Leonidas and the heroic three hundred had died at Thermopylae to give Athenians time to evacuate their city. Without Sparta's help, the Athenians would have lost at Plataea. The hatemongers, Ephialtes and Pericles, would destroy the unity of Greece and render the Hellas vulnerable to Persian attack. The issue, as he expressed it, was survival. He appealed to the assembly to give him four thousand men whom he could lead to victory in Sparta.

The president put the question. The majority was still under the spell of Cimon. He was granted his request. In this second great debate between the conservatives and the liberals, Ephialtes and Pericles were defeated again. Within three days, four thousand Athenians "fell in" and marched to Peloponnesia under the command of Cimon. Ephialtes and Pericles were not invited to participate.

The incorporeal god, Fate, had always been an overpowering god to the Greeks, even though he was not anthropomorphic, as most of their gods were. Zeus sometimes had to succumb to Fate's will. Even the educated, the most sophisticated, were, to some extent, fatalists. The events of the next few weeks probably convinced Pericles that fate's capricious course was still set to favor the people's cause.

Perhaps it was a professional runner or an advance horseman who brought the incredible news from Peloponnesus before Cimon's army of four thousand returned from its Spartan "mission of mercy." As much as Cimon must have hated it, he would have to attempt to prepare the populace for the red-faced return of his troops. The word spread fast. Cimon and his four thousand were headed home, not crowned with glory, but deluged with embarrassment and confusion. The Spartans had changed their minds and decided they did not want Athens' help. Seeing such a large foreign army present in their land, they became apprehensive about the well-known ambitious nature of the Athenians and feared they might decide to conquer Sparta rather than help suppress its serfs. Also, it was said, many Athenians had found that in fighting Sparta's enemies they would not be fighting slaves but fellow Greeks who were being oppressed. There had arisen much murmur against the Spartans in the Athenian ranks. So the Spartans sent the Athenian army home. Pericles and Ephialtes might have roared with self-righteous "I told you so" laughter had they not been so angrily disgusted with Cimon's stupidity.

The first of the lusterless troops trekked into the city, disbanded, and melted quietly into their scattered homes. A few curious Athenians stood on the sides of the street and watched them, but no one cheered. Cimon slipped back into the city inconspicuously. The flame of resentment among the citizens was fanned by the leaders of the liberal party. It was Ephialtes' and Pericles' chance to strike—and strike hard. The majority of the people were furious at Cimon and his friends. He had been the instrument of Athens' degrading insult at the hands of the Spartans. Ephialtes and Pericles had been right. The ignorant and duplicitous Spartans were not their allies and could not be trusted. Even the majority of the men who had marched with Cimon returned mortified and disillusioned with their gullible, Spartan-loving leader.

When Cimon, responding to the demands of the oligarchs, sought the assembly's reconsideration of the action downgrading the Areopagus, he was hooted down. The time had come. The people could visualize Cimon as a despot and a threat to their liberties. Ephialtes put the motion; Pericles seconded it. They smote Cimon with the ostrakon, and he was banished from Athens for ten years.

Ephialtes, leader of the liberals, took over as Chief General. Pericles was elected general of his tribe at thirty-one and became Ephialtes' strong right arm. Pericles proudly fixed the purple plume to his helmet. Then fate struck another violent blow. Ephialtes was murdered during the night by a paid assassin who stabbed him with a knife in the back.

The assassin was apprehended and admitted that he had been paid one thousand drachmae for the job. However, the money had been handed to him through a bush in the graveyard at night, and he could not identify his employer.

The head of the state of Athens was dead. The citizens sorrowfully trekked to Pynx Hill to choose a successor. The liberal party was even stronger now, being solidified by what was obviously the political assassination of their leader. The martyr's mantle fell on the shoulders of his lieutenant, Pericles. At thirty-one in 461 B.C. he became the leader of the Athenians.

Five years later, Pericles induced the assembly to reprieve Cimon so he could use him to help secure a peace treaty with Sparta. In Pericles' first sixteen years at Athens' helm, he did not attempt to use the club of ostracism to retain power. His wisdom and golden tongue gave him unparalleled powers of persuasion, and he considered himself too noble to resort to the elimination of competitors. He could handle them at the ballot box. But when one Thucydides (not the historian) attacked his building program and banished his best friend, Damon, he too assembled the citizens and passed out the pottery. Thucydides was driven out of town.

Rockefeller money constructed a replica of the Stoa of Attalus on the agora in Athens. The original was built in the second century B.C. It serves as a fascinating museum, or home for the Muses,[30] and preserves priceless artifacts uncovered on the agora. Among the wondrous objects are shards with the names of Xanthippus and Themistocles scratched on them. Ballots were cast twenty-five hundred years ago by Athenian citizens fighting the fear of tyranny.

Pericles avoided the scythe of the ostrakon for thirty

---

[30]A Muse was one of the nine sister goddesses in Greek mythology presiding over poetry, music, dance, and the arts in general.

years—the only top Athenian leader of the fifth century to escape banishment. At least in a democracy, it took three thousand votes to lose one's political head. In the monarchies of the day, it took only one vote—the king's. And some think politics in the United States is rough!

8

The Trial of a City

Lesbos, known for centuries as the "island of the blessed," was the island of the cursed for a period of twenty-four hours in the summer of 428 B.C. It is a verdant, wooded island in the northeast Aegean in sight of the Turkish coast. It sits just off the course of the tedious tourist who steams unconsciously by it en route from Ephesus to Istanbul.

A tourist who adventures to Lesbos can swim with a few escapist world-wandering artists in the colony at Mythemne on the northern shores of Lesbos. They can hunt wild game in the hills and join in the wine-washed revelry of the Ceremony of the Bull, one celebration that survived the pagan purge by Christianity, hanging onto the heritage of the Minoan civilization that permeated the Greek world two thousand years before Christ. They can wander the ancient dirt roads bisecting the ruins of Thermi, a contemporary city of Troy about 1,200 B.C., a city carefully planned in the shape of a fish bone. At Thermi they can bathe in the thermal springs and then ride donkeys past quarries of black marble back to Mytilene, the city that has been the capitol of Lesbos since time runneth not. There they can quaff their thirst with some of the best anise-flavored ouzo in Greece. Only the petrified trees have been there longer than the city of Mytilene. It is a lazy, whitewashed wraith of a town lolling in the Aegean sun at the rounded head of an enclosed harbor reached by a long-necked channel craning upward from the sea. Over the centuries it has been conquered by an endless procession of invaders, but it has hovered near death only once—when the Athenian assembly put it on trial on the Pynx.

Today, Lesbos lies peacefully in the shadow of its ancient eminence. With its prestigious city-states of Methymna and Mytilene and the latter's sizable navy, it was a significant force in the Greek world of the fifth century B.C. After Athens' infantry won the battle of Marathon in 490 B.C., and its navy the battle of Salamis a decade later, Lesbos became an ally of Athens in the Delian League formed in 478 B.C. Athens' general that year, Aristides the Just, chaired the panhellenic conference, which met at Delos and formed the confederation (a sort of NATO) to defend the Greeks against any future attacks by the imperialistic Persians. Sparta and its satellites did not join. At the organization ceremonies, the remarkable Aristides, hailed for his integrity and representing revered Athens, savior of the Hellas, expressed the deep devotion of Athens' allies when he dropped iron bars into the Aegean and participants swore on oath that they would be loyal to the league until iron floated.

Fifty years later the oligarchic leaders of Lesbos decided that iron could float. They revolted against Athens and a league that was no longer a league but an Athenian empire. Pericles had transformed the federation into a collection of satellites paying tribute to Athens whose incomparable navy, in return, provided wooden-wall defense for all Greece against the Persian empire.

The Athenians were furious with Lesbos because it was one of the members of the league that had never been reduced by Athens to a vassal status. Lesbos and Chios were the two states that had remained partners rather than subjects of Athens. They did not pay dues. They supplied ships and men to fight beside Athenians whenever the Persians futilely gestured militarily toward the West. But they feared that sometime Athens would subjugate them as it had the other islands and cities. At least its rich men, its oligarchs, nursed this fear. Athens had taught Lesbos democracy and supervised the establishment of democratic governments in all the cities of the league, given them assemblies, people's courts, and freedom of expression. It had given them democratic constitutions whether they wanted them or not. And, as long as the democratic parties, supported by the people, reigned, Athens granted them supervised autonomy. But, when the aristocracy intervened and took command and replaced the democratic institutions with oligarchy, Athens had been ruthless. Athens policed the league. It insisted on making the world safe for democracy.

It was the fourth year of the Peloponnesian War pitting Sparta and its allies against Athens and its empire. It was the fourth summer that Spartan soldiers had invaded Attica and laid its fields bare as the citizens of Attica huddled inside Athens' walls. The fourth year, Athens' navy had sailed forth and conquered port cities vital to Sparta, threatening its eventual isolation and starvation. It was the third year of a horrible, decimating plague that had mowed through Athens like a scourging scythe, killing at least twenty-five percent of its population and undermining its morale. It was a bad time for a friend to turn foe.

Athens received intelligence that Mytilene, which previously had been aligned with Athens against Sparta, was going to switch sides. It sent forty ships to Mytilene and nipped the revolt in the bud. An armistice was reached, and Athens left a naval garrison in the harbor under the command of General Paches to keep the peace.

Mytilene's leaders were only chafing and marking time while its diplomats surreptitiously headed for Sparta to seek its aid in a renewed attempt to sever its alliance with Athens. Sparta directed the Mytilenian agent to meet with its leaders at Olympia, where the games had interrupted the war.

Olympia's peaceful, luxuriant panorama today belies the political conspiracy that often permeated the temples and palaestrae while the athletes performed. Representatives of the Spartans and their allies assembled in the columned Temple of Zeus to hear the appeal of the unnamed delegate from Lesbos sent to induce them to support Mytilene's revolt. The temple stood in the center of a cluster of buildings that formed the sacred center of the city. The base of the temple still rests there today with its grey-fluted columns sprawled on the ground in segments around its perimeter, lying there as they fell hundreds of years ago. Across the street from the temple stood the gymnasium, the school, and the workshop of the famous sculptor, Phidias, and just south of it the large hotel where the wealthy attending the games took lodging. To the north nestled the smaller temple to Hera, Zeus' shrewish, jealous wife, and beyond, stretching eastward, the treasuries of the various Greek cities storing the gifts brought to honor the gods and to provide the priests of the games the money to sponsor the quadrenniel festival. In front of the Temple of Zeus, the stone structure still stands where the Olympic torch was lighted then and is still lighted today from the flames of the burning olive oil.

Behind the speaker of Lesbos towered the gigantic statue of the sitting Zeus, sculpted by Phidias only about twenty-five years before. Pausanius, who toured through the temple more than six hundred years later, wrote that seeing the statue was a "spiritual experience."

In the account written by Thucydides, the earnest man from Mytilene reviewed the history of his city's relationship with Athens:

> The alliance between ourselves and the Athenians began when you withdrew from the war against the Persians and they remained to finish the business. But we did not become allies of the Athenians for the subjugation of the Hellenes, but allies of the Hellenes for their liberation from the Medes.[31]

He stated that Athens, by its subjugation of other cities, had become stronger and Mytilene weaker. Never had the old balance of power principle been stated better. Some perceptive scholar has said that no one has written anything new about history since Thucydides. The age-old justification for aggression was action taken in self-defense—strike before being struck. Thucydides went on:

> Lesbos may appear far off, but when help is wanted she will be found near enough. It is not in Attica that the war will be decided, as some imagine, but in the countries by which Attica is supported; and the Athenian revenue is drawn from the allies, and will become still larger if they reduce us; as not only will no other state revolt, but our resources will be added to theirs, and we shall be treated worse than those that were enslaved before. But if you will frankly support us, you will add to your side a state that has a large navy, which is your great want; you will smooth the way to the overthrow of the Athenians by depriving them of their allies, who will be greatly encouraged to come over; and you will free yourselves from the accusation made against you of not supporting insurrection. In short, only show yourselves as liberators, and you may count upon having the advantage in the war.

---

[31]Thucydides, *The Landmark Thucydides: A Comprehensive Guide to the Peloponnesian War*, ed. Robert B. Strassler, introduction by Victor D. Hanson (New York: Free Press, 1996), 163.

> Respect, therefore, both the hopes placed in you by the Hellenes, and Olympian Zeus in whose temple we stand virtually as suppliants; become the allies and defenders of the Mytilenians, and do not sacrifice us, who put our lives in jeopardy for a cause in which general good will result to all from our success, and still more general harm if we fail through your refusing to help us. Be the men that the Hellenes think you, and that our fears desire.[32]

The Spartans were persuaded. They invited Lesbos into their league and promised to assist its revolt. They waited, however, until the next summer and then assembled forty ships and dispatched them to Lesbos.

Athens was aware of what was going on. It was not as exhausted as the Lesbians thought. They immediately sent one thousand infantry soldiers to Lesbos on ships they rowed themselves and arrived in the autumn several months before the Spartans even launched their fleet. They built a wall around Lesbos and completely blockaded the city. The Spartans took their time on the way, stopping at various islands. Before they arrived, the Mytilenians surrendered to the Athenian force and accepted the terms of their captors. Athens was to have the right to act as it saw fit with regard to the people of Mytilene, and the army was allowed to enter the city; the Mytilenians were to send representatives to Athens to put their case, and until these emissaries returned, General Paches was not to imprison, enslave, or kill any of the population. The Spartans arrived in the area about seven days after the surrender of Mytilene. They decided not to tangle with the Athenians and returned to Pelopponesus.

When the representatives of Mytilene arrived in Athens, they got short shrift. The citizens met on the Hill of Pynx in an assembly seething with animosity. While their former ally had been revolting, they had been burying their

---

[32]Ibid., 165.

hundreds felled by the plague. The Spartan infantry had been laying desolate the countryside of Attica, and Athens' main fleets had been battling Sparta and her allies in various areas of the Greek world. The citizens were sick and tired, their treasury was running low, and scores of them were still succumbing to the drastic disease. Hatred for the state they had treated as partners was rampant.

Pericles, their serene and intellectual leader, had been replaced by Cleon, an ignorant, uneducated, demagogic hide-tanner with a fiery gift for oratory. He was as wild, eloquent, unprincipled, and heartless as Hitler. He slapped the myrtle wreath on his hot head, mounted the rostrum, and shouted for the punishment of the disloyal devils of Lesbos. He moved that all of its male citizens be killed and that its women and children be sold into slavery. The mad mob roared its approval.

Diodotus, a cultured man of intellect and breeding, took the rostrum and tried to dissuade the crowd but was shouted down and the motion carried. Cleon immediately dispatched a ship from Piraeus to Lesbos with orders for General Paches to implement the will of the assembly. The trireme rowed out of the harbor, hoisted its sails, and was on its way to deliver the murderous ultimatum.

Overnight the tempers of the Athenians cooled when they contemplated the unprecedented cruelty of their decree. At the bidding of Diodotus, another meeting of the assembly was called by hoisting the flag on the Pynx, and again the male citizens climbed the hill to hear the debate and deliberate. Cleon again commandeered the rostrum first. Thucydides states that he was "remarkable among the Athenians for the violence of his character." Aristophanes, the playwright, later described him as a "craven, profligate hound." Cleon put all the force of his perverted personality into a long, haranguing, and bombastic speech. He was furious with the vacillation of his people. His speech is remarkable for its parallelism with the tortured philosophy of many today.

For too long Cleon, the ambitious politician, had been forced to simmer in the shadow of the intellectual Pericles, and now he had to endure the self-acclaimed superiority of learned men like Diodotus, who would follow him on the platform. His own lack of education caused him to lash out against writers, teachers, and Sophists. For years he had suffered the slights of the cultured class. Now he was the vote-getter, the leader, by virtue of his bull will and ability to talk—his guts, gall, and demagoguery. His irresponsible promises to supply the masses with anything they wanted that the formerly fat treasury of the city could provide. The rich and the learned would be laid low and he, the lowborn man of the people, would show them how to rule themselves and their empire. He proceeded for a time with a diatribe against intellectuals and then returned to the treachery of the Mytileneans.

Pericles, after having led and served his people successfully for many years, had been able to chide them firmly when they threatened to act foolishly. He had done it on the Pynx when their spirits were low after the first winter of demoralizing plague and they wanted to appease the Spartans and end the war. But Pericles could reprove gracefully, maintaining the dignity and ego of his listener, and he had thirty years of successful leadership to back his remonstrances. Cleon, with a year of undistinguished command, was trying to play Pericles. There was a difference between a stinking hide-tanner with a big voice and glib tongue and a scion of the great Alcmaeonid family. Aristocrats such as the Roosevelts, the Kennedys, and the Alcmaeonids always do better with the masses than one of their own.

If Cleon had lost his audience with his tactless remonstrances, he was winning them back with his dramatic account of Mytilene's treachery. Confident and callous, Cleon proceeded:

> Our mistake has been to distinguish the Mytilenians as we have done: had they been long ago treated like the rest; they never would have so far forgotten themselves, human nature being as surely made arrogant by consideration, as it is awed by firmness. Let them now, therefore, be punished as their crime requires, and do not, while you condemn the aristocracy, absolve the people. This is certain, that all attacked you without distinction, although they might have come over to us, and been now again in possession of their city. But no, they thought it safer to throw in their lot with the aristocracy and so joined their rebellion! . . .
>
> No hope, therefore, must be held out to the Mytilenians, that their rhetoric may inspire or money purchase the mercy due to human infirmity. Their offense was not involuntary, but of malice and deliberate; and mercy is only for unwilling offenders. I therefore now, as before, persist against your reversing your first decision, or giving way to the three failings most fatal to empire—pity, sentiment, and indulgence.[33]

It is little wonder that Plato, who was born the year this speech was given, grew to deplore democracy. Minds and leadership such as Cleon's soured him on government by the people and motivated him to frame his ideal of government in the *Republic* where the leader would be a philosopher-king and only those would participate in government who had had thirty years of schooling followed by fifteen years of actual experience in the practical world. If he passed all those tests and had reached the age of fifty, he could be considered for public office.

After Cleon's speech, the citizens munched on their cheese and sipped their wine as Diodotus took the rostrum. The scholarly Diodotus knew he could not match the oratory of Cleon. He would have to appeal to reason. He spoke with controlled earnestness, flaring off for a moment his

---

[33]Ibid., 178.

contempt for Cleon's witless approach and then leaning on logic:

> I do not blame the persons who have reopened the case of the Mytilenians, nor do I approve the protests which we have heard against important questions being frequently debated. I think the two things most opposed to good counsel are haste and passion; haste usually goes hand in hand with folly, passion with coarseness and narrowness of mind. . . .
>
> Only consider what a blunder you would commit in doing as Cleon recommends. As things are at present, in all the cities The People is our friend, and either does not revolt with the oligarchy, or, if forced to do so, becomes at once the enemy of the insurgents; so that in the war with the hostile city you have the masses on your side. But if you butcher The People of Mytilene, who have nothing to do with the revolt, and who, as soon as they got arms, of their own motion surrendered the city, first you will commit the crime of killing your benefactors; and next you will play directly into the hands of the higher classes, who when they induce their cities to rise, will immediately have The People on their side, through your having announced in advance the same punishment for those who are guilty and for those who are not. . . .
>
> Confess, therefore, that this is the wisest course, and without conceding too much either to pity or to indulgence, by neither of which motives do I any more than Cleon wish you to be influenced, upon the plain merits of the case before you, be persuaded by me to try calmly those of the Mytilenians whom Paches sent off as guilty, and to leave the rest undisturbed.[34]

Diodotus handed the wreath to the clerk and took his seat on the wooden bench on the front row. It was a blistering hot summer day and the grass on the Pynx had turned brown. The vote was called for; the citizens of Athens raised their hands and they were counted.

---

[34]Ibid., 179, 182.

The vote was a stirring revelation. Pericles, the statesman; Anaxagoras, Protagoras, Democritus, and Socrates, the philosophers; Hippocrates, the physician-scientist; Aeschylus, Sophocles, and Euripides, the playwrights; Herodotus, the historian; and other cerebrators of that enlightened generation had *started* the clock of man's mind ticking. They *had*, for a time, taught the people to think. The motion of Diodotus was passed. It was a thrilling thing to see a mob turned from riot to reason. Diodotus had done it.

The end of the story cannot be better phrased than in the succinct words of Thucydides, who was alive at the time:

> Another trireme was at once sent off in haste, for fear that the first might reach Lesbos in the interval, and the city be found destroyed; the first ship having about a day and a night's start. Wine and barley-cakes were provided for the vessel by the Mytilenian ambassadors, and great promises made if they arrived in time. . . . Luckily they met with no contrary wind, and the first ship making no haste upon so horrid an errand, while the second pressed on in the manner described, the first arrived so little before them that Paches had only just had time to read the decree, and to prepare to execute the sentence, when the second put into port and prevented the massacre. The danger of Mytilene had indeed been great.[35]

---

[35]Ibid., 183.

9

The Trial of the Eight Generals

In 431 B.C., the Peloponnesian War matching Sparta and its Peloponnesian League against Athens and its Delian League commenced. Pericles was still in command of the greatest empire on earth, and Sparta was the cautious custodian of the independence of the Greeks who envied and feared Athens. But Pericles died in 429 B.C.; with him died his plan for a quick victory.

The war proceeded periodically for ten years of summer fighting. The Greeks had the good sense to fight only during the clement summer weather. Combatants hustled home in the winter. There was no sense in slamming swords, slinging spears, and ramming ships during the uncomfortable temperatures of winter.

Athens had been achieving a slight edge in the conflict, thanks to its incomparable navy. And in 421 B.C., General Nicias, inept as he was, negotiated a treaty of peace with Sparta and its allies.

Unfortunately for Athens and the history of mankind, Alcibiades, the brilliant, handsome, unprincipled, and uncontrollably ambitious foster son of Pericles, started the war again to promote his own power. In 415 B.C., while Athens was sparring satisfactorily with Sparta, Alcibiades, goaded by a psychopathic lust for fame, talked the assembly into attempting to conquer Syracuse, the Greek city, second only in size and significance to Athens. Syracuse was located on the island of Sicily. Ruins today hint of its ancient glory.

Athens lost that bout in 413 B.C. partly because its citizens, in the middle of the campaign, stupidly banished Alcibiades, their only general who might have pulled it off. The Athenians, during the period of their democracy, always made sure that civilian power maintained the ascendancy over military. Military generals, believe it or not, were elected and deposed by popular vote. Fortunately, the Athenians' forefathers had learned the art of war well from the professionals: Miltiades, Themistocles, and Cimon. Pericles had maintained the tradition and training, and the sons had learned from the fathers. But a general's tenure was very insecure. Athens was strictly a citizen army and navy, commanded by the most popular politicians. In the tragic campaign at Syracuse, Athens sacrificed thousands of men and hundreds of ships and depleted its treasury.

Alcibiades, unable to go home, took up residence in Sparta and retired to the bed of an absent, fighting Spartan king's wife, and the war ground on. Athens and Sparta exchanged blows all over Greece, from Thrace to southern Peloponnesus. They warred through the islands of the Aegean Sea. In 411 B.C. democracy was replaced in Athens by the rule of the Four Hundred. Athens recalled the swashbuckling Alcibiades to take command, and the year closed with Athenian victories in the Aegean and at Abydos on the Hellespont.

There the account of the war by the great historian Thucydides ends, and the baton of narrative in the relentless relay of history was passed to Xenophon. In his *Hellenica*, he relates the incident of the trial of the six generals. For Xenophon, man of action, cavalry commander, and infantry immortal, to take up the stylus and write was appropriate, for he was born in 431 B.C., the year the war began. He began to write *Hellenica* at twenty, the year he became a citizen of Athens.

He tells of the fall of the Four Hundred and the reestablishment of a modified democracy in Athens under the leadership of General Theramanes, a politician nicknamed Buskin. The buskin was a boot worn on the stage by tragic actors of Athens. It could be worn on either foot and was applied to Theramanes to characterize his ability to shift easily from the democratic to the autocratic party and back —a political hermaphrodite. Then Xenophon described the battle of Arginusae where the alleged crime of the eight generals was committed. The Arginusae is a group of islands floating close by the eastern shore of the island of Lesbos in the Aegean Sea—an hour's rowing distance from Lesbos' capitol city of Mytilene, which today lolls lazily in the Aegean sun.

Athens' navy, operating in the eastern Aegean, was placed under the command of Conon, who was a capable, nonpolitical, and professional naval officer.

The incorrigible Alcibiades was gone again—re-ostracized by an erratic assembly that could not cope with his unsettling genius. They could not do with or without him. They needed his generalship but panicked every time he became strong enough to conquer Athens' masses with his charm, competence, and overweening ego. The code of

Cleisthenes, destroy all potential dictators, was still strong stuff in the minds of the individualistic Athenians, even in the midst of a death-rattling national emergency.

Commanding the enemy fleet in nearby waters was one Callicratidas, a somewhat civilized and engaging Spartan who had temporarily replaced the renowned Lysander, eventual conqueror of Athens. Lysander had already made a deal with the Persians by which Cyrus, the Younger, was contributing substantially to the financial support of the Spartan navy. Athens had saved Sparta at Marathon and Salamis from domination by the Persians, but those self-centered, isolationists from the mountains of Peloponnesus had no appreciation and no loyalty for their fellow Greeks. They constituted an uneducated and separate tribe, characterized chiefly by muscle, treachery, and stupidity. They had not advanced since the lofty Lycurgus schooled them in the art of ignorance three hundred years before.

Athens had its individual traitors, but, to its everlasting credit, it never sought the aid of foreigners against its fellow Greeks. It is poetic and moral justice that Athens is the great city of Greece today, while Sparta does not even possess the foundation of a ruin to evidence that it ever existed. A narrow culture based solely on militarism does not survive. Spectacular Sparta is not on the tourist trail and properly so.

But Callicratidas was an interesting character—for a Spartan. When he heard that Conon, the Athenian commander, was gearing for maneuvers in the eastern Aegean, he sent him this cavalier message: "I am going to put a stop to your fornication with the sea. She belongs to me."[36] The Spartans did have a wholesome attitude toward sex. The Spartan fleet clashed with the outnumbered Athenians, and the latter retreated into the harbor at Mytilene, where Calli-

---

[36]Xenophon, *A History of My Times (Hellenica)*, trans. Rex Warner (Harmondsworth, England: Penguin Books, 1981).

cratidas locked them in and blockaded them.

One Athenian trireme escaped to Athens and reported the defeat. The Athenians were low on triremes, but finally by melting some of their treasures into money, they outfitted 110 triremes and started for Lesbos to break the blockade. In order to man that many, Athens had to free hundreds of slaves and give citizenship to hundreds of aliens to call them to the oars. They picked up thirty ships from allies on the way and proceeded to the islands off Arginusae where they anchored for a night. The following day they moved out and met the attacking forces of Callicratidas.

Eight of the generals of Athens commanded ships in the battle. Pericles, the Younger, love child of Pericles and Aspasia, was one of the eight and had fifteen ships under his flag. The Athenians won the day, ramming, sinking, or disabling sixty-nine Spartan vessels. Callicratidas fell overboard and drowned when his ship was rammed. The remaining Spartans fled to Chios and elsewhere, followed by the fifty of their fleet which had bottled Conon's squadron up in the harbor. That freed Conon's ships and they joined up with the remainder of the Athenian fleet.

Twenty-five Athenian ships had been sunk or disabled. Forty-seven operating Athenian triremes were assigned to pick up the crews of the disabled ships, while the remainder chased futilely after the fleeing Spartans. But a violent storm arose sometime after the battle—no one seems to know just how soon after—and the rescuing forty-seven triremes failed to pick up the survivors who, consequently, perished in the sea.

The failure to rescue was the crime for which six of the eight generals were tried by the assembly when they returned to Athens. Two of the generals who had participated in the battle did not return to the city. They escaped the most foolhardy and illegal prosecution ever conducted in the history of the ancient democracy.

As usual, the Hill of the Pynx was where the major action occurred. The citizens met and sat on the three-thousand-seat benches and on the ground when the seats ran out. The word had preceded the generals that they had left the survivors of the twenty-five ships to die. At the first meeting, the assembly summarily deposed all of the generals, except Conon who had been bottled up in the harbor at Mytilene.

Then, for a day, the action shifted to the agora, to a court of people's jurors to hear charges against one general for having public money in his possession and for misconduct as a general. The charge was brought by a leading popular politician—popular largely because he operated a relief fund—something Solon and Pericles would not have condoned. In Solon's time, a man made his own living or he did not eat. In Pericles' time, what we called "creeping socialism" in the 1930s had crept to public works projects, such as building the Parthenon, to provide for the unemployed. By this time in Athens, liberalism had been advanced by aggressive politicians to the humanitarian institution of relief. The politician succeeds who promises the most for the least. The state owed a man a living whether he worked or not, when depression, imposed by a long war, made it easier to dole out obols[37] for relief than drachmae for public building. Anyway, this popular politician addressed the jury and the general was imprisoned. Xenophon, the historian, does not suggest whether the evidence justified conviction or not. That conviction inspired an attack on the other generals. Another politician addressed charges to the Council of Five Hundred (fifty from each of the ten tribes). They constituted the most powerful governmental entity in

---

[37]An obol, the smallest monetary unit in ancient Greek, was a coin or weight equal to one-sixth drachma. It has been estimated that a single man could live on two obols a day in late fifth-century Athens.

the city because they prepared the agenda for the assembly and rough-drafted all legislation to be considered by it. The speaker recommended that all six of the returned generals be prosecuted for misconduct. He urged they be tried, not before the people's juries where those accused were supposed to be tried under the law, but before the assembly.

The code of criminal procedure in Athens requiring that all accused be brought before the court was not chiseled in stone. It had been codified by custom during the reign of Pericles, but there was no Pericles present to persuade the council to comply with the law. He had died twenty-three years before. And the Supreme Court, the Areopagus, had been shorn of its supervisory and appellate powers and could not enforce the legal procedure.

The agitated council granted the motion that the generals be tried by the mob—the assembly. The action shifted back to Pynx Hill. The curious citizens abandoned their farms, flocks, wineries, boats, quarries, and shops, and swarmed onto the slopes, turning the Pynx into an anthill of feverish activity.

The generals had been spreading the word that it was not they who had abandoned the survivors, but the captains of the forty-seven ships left to conduct the rescue, while the generals pursued their duty by attempting to follow the retreating Spartan fleet. Theramanes, former general, avid politician, seeking return to power, had been one of the ships' captains left to pick up the men clinging to their wounded vessels. He was the most vigorous and articulate of the accusers.

He pointed out that the generals had changed their story. At first they had sent a letter to the council claiming that the cause of the failure to rescue the men was the intervention of the storm. The letter had said nothing about the derelictions of the trierarchs.[38] Now they were trying to blame the captains. Why had they not said that in their letter? They were responsible.

Each of the six generals was then allowed to speak in his own defense, including Pericles, the son of Pericles. Pericles, the Younger, was probably not as eloquent as his father, though he was about twenty-one when his father died and should have received good training from a father who loved him profoundly.

Pericles had neglected his other two boys born of his first and unloved wife. His oldest son, Xanthippus, named after his grandfather, proved to be a disobedient, rebellious, and dissolute brat, who accomplished nothing but the embarrassment of his father. Paralos was loved by his father and was a so-so son, with no special ability or character. They both died in their twenties from the plague of 430 B.C.

But Pericles, son of Aspasia, was something else. He had the superior mind and body of his two extraordinary parents and, as evidenced by his election to the exalted position of general, marked him as one of the ten leading citizens of Athens during his term. Pericles thought his immortality rested in the hands of his one surviving citizen-son.

If Pericles, the Younger, held a touch of his father's oratorical magic, he had little chance to use it. The assembly violated another section of Athens' code of criminal procedure. They would not permit the six generals to speak for the full time an accused was entitled to speak before the jury courts. Speakers were timed in the courts and the assembly by clay pots used as clocks. They varied in size and were filled with water. The plug was pulled when the speaker began and when the water was gone, the speaker was stopped. They had the equivalent of hour water vessels and

---

[38]A trierarch was the captain in charge of a trireme.

half hour and others. At the trial of the generals, the pots were only partially filled and the water ran out fast. When sound procedural law crumbles, substantive law falls.

The generals argued that the task of rescue had been given to the trierarchs while they pursued the enemy. But they said they were not going to lie. They produced witnesses, steersmen, and sailors who confirmed their claims, and their arguments were proving effective. Assemblymen were listening and nodding. A number of citizens rose from the grass and the wooden benches and offered to provide bail for them. But the sun had set and dusk descended, and it would be impossible to count the hands if they voted. It was decided to adjourn and authorize the council to propose the type of trial the generals should have.

Before the meeting of the council, the festival of Apituria intervened. It was a family festival where fathers and mothers met together with their children. The politicians plotted. Several families were persuaded, probably paid, to appear at the festivities dressed in black with their hair close shaven, pretending to be kinsmen of the men who had been sacrificed in the battle. The sympathy of the celebrants was aroused and feeling rose against the generals.

One Callixeinus, a gifted speaker, was bribed to attack the generals at the meeting of the council. The council called a meeting of the assembly. The trial resumed on the Pynx. The council resolved that since the accusing speeches and the generals' speeches in their own defense had been heard that the Athenians should now vote by tribes.

They provided two voting urns. If the majority of the potsherds declared the generals guilty for failing to pick up the men, they would be punished with death and their property would be confiscated by the state and a tenth part of it consecrated to the goddess Athena.

This was the resolution offered by the council. One citizen, aged Euryptolemus, cousin of the senior Pericles, intervened with a summons to the effect that the proposed resolution was unconstitutional and could not be legally considered by the assembly. But the excited mass of citizens shouted him down, roaring their right to do as they pleased, for they were the people, the source of all constitutional power, the fountain of legal rights and responsibilities. In the face of the riotous rabble, the summons was withdrawn.

A presiding committee conducted the meetings of the assembly. The parliamentary rules required that a representative of the committee present the motion for a vote. Some of them demurred on the grounds of its illegality, but a tumult arose from the crowd and threats were issued, demanding the presentation of the motion. In terror, all the members of the presiding committee (except one) acceded to the uproar. He sat on a bench in front of the concrete rostrum from which Solon, Themistocles, and Pericles had addressed the citizens numberless times as they formulated the foundations of democracy.

The other committeemen asked their dissident member, one Socrates, to make the motion, and he became the cynosure of the crowd's attention. The generals fixed their eyes on him with hope, for he was known as a man of independence and courage. Pericles, the Younger, watched him and recalled the kindly, unorthodox, and iconoclastic philosopher who had been his teacher in his youth—a man loved, platonically but profoundly, by his mother, Aspasia. The philosopher was old now, sixty-two, and the well-known twinkle in his eyes had changed to anger. He still wore the frayed tunic. His bare feet stirred the dust as he sat. His big head and broad ugly face appeared set in a firm resolve; his pug nose and flared nostrils seemed to snort silently at the entire proceedings. His barrel chest swelled as he inhaled, and he squared his still powerful, broad shoulders and refused to make or join in the presentation of the motion. He declared that he would do nothing that was contrary to law.

The mob shouted his name in derision—"Socrates!" The meddlesome, questioning philosopher with his own new gods would not be permitted to obstruct the will of the people. He remained firm and stood alone among his quaking committee colleagues, and the assembly overruled him and the motion was put.

The floodgates of debate flew open again. Euryptolemus, Pericles' cousin, rose to speak. Plutarch remembered Euryptolemus five hundred years later, not for this speech, but for the fact that Pericles, the austere, hard-working statesman, who did not socialize publicly, made one exception. He attended the wedding of his cousin Euryptolemus. Euryptolemus' appeal has been preserved by Xenophon:

> Men of Athens, . . . If you will follow my advice and do what is just and right and what will best enable you to learn the truth and best preserve you from finding out later to your sorrow that it is you yourselves who have been guilty—guilty to the gods and guilty to yourselves. Now my advice is this: give these men at least one day, if not more, to speak in their own defense, and put your trust not in others but in yourselves. In this way you cannot be deceived either by me or anybody else and you will be able, with full knowledge, to inflict on the guilty any punishment you like, either on all of them together or on each one separately.
>
> Men of Athens, you have won a great and fortunate victory. Do not act as though you were smarting under the ignominy of defeat. Do not be so unreasonable as not to recognize that some things are in the hand of heaven. These men are helpless; do not condemn them for treachery. They were simply unable, because of the storm, to do what they had been ordered to do. Indeed, it would be a very much fairer thing to crown these victors with garlands than to punish them, at the instigation of rogues, with death.[39]

---

[39]Ibid., 89-90, 92-93.

Euryptolemus then moved that each of the men should be given a separate trial in accordance with the decree of Cannonus. The council's motion, of course, was to try them together and decide their fate by one vote. A vote was taken adopting Euryptolemus' motion; then further debate ensued; a reconsideration moved and a second and final vote taken which approved the plan of the council. Then they hastily voted on the guilt or innocence of the eight generals—the six present and the two absent—and found them guilty, and the six generals were put to death.

In one generation, from Pericles to Pericles, the Younger, democracy's judicial system had collapsed. The fatherly force of Pericles' persuasive voice was no longer heard in the land. Without the wisdom, personality, and leadership of the great general, the devil in democracy took command. Mob violence replaced the rule of law. The echo of Pericles' still voice could not save his son.

Within a few days, recrimination, repentance, and regret fell heavily on the hearts of the hundreds who had stood on the hill and intemperately executed their fellow citizens in violation of the law. In a fit of reaction, they arrested Callixeinus, who had persuaded the council to push the prosecution. He and others arrested escaped before trial. Later, Callixeinus returned to the city, but he was loathed by the people and died of starvation.

Greeks are incorrigible individualists. The pyrotechnics that exploded on the Pynx were symptomatic of the inveterate Greek individualism, characterizing the long history of its people. In ancient times, they were divided by ruggedly mountainous country into separate autonomous city states, which continuously fought each other in fratricidal wars. Even when communication among the cities improved, the Greeks, husbanding a comparatively barren land, depended on trade with foreigners for economic survival rather than each other. Corinth, Aegina, Athens, and Megara, for example, were constant economic competitors for the grain of Egypt and the lands surrounding the Black Sea.

The ancient Olympic games, commenced in 776 B.C., demonstrated the individuality of the Greek nature. City-states did not compete in the races, the wrestles, and the decathlon. Individuals competed. There was no accumulation of gold or silver medals for any city. The individual, not the state, won or lost. There was no city "team," no team training, registration, or city subsidy. No one stood and saluted a flag, or sang the Star Spangled Attica, or the Spartan hymn. There was no city uniform. In some events, they competed in the nude. You could not tell an Athenian from a Corinthian and no loud-speaking system announced the city that the athlete represented because he represented no city. It was the individual athlete who was honored. When he won, he became a panhellenic hero, respected and revered by all Greeks in all cities. Sometimes the day after the Olympics ended, the respective Greek cities went back to besieging each other mercilessly in total war.

THE ACROPOLIS

10

Athenian Politics

In 444 B.C. Pericles took his first vacation in at least sixteen years. After being gone several weeks, he returned to Athens to find that he had been deposed as Chief General. One Thucydides, the leader of the oligarchic, conservative party, was governing the city. Construction on the Parthenon had been stopped.

An investigation had revealed that during Pericles' sixteen years in power his organization had allowed thousands of thetes[40] to register and vote in the election of generals and other top officials. Solon's four classes of citizens still existed officially. The four classes were divided on the basis of property ownership. The members of the two upper

---

[40] A thete was the fourth and lowest property-class in the Solonian census, and had an annual income of less than 200 bushels of corn, wine, or oil. The thetes could not hold office but served as rowers and marines in the Athenian fleet.

classes, the pentacosiomedimnoi[41] and the hippeis[42] were the only ones allowed to vote for the top political offices until 457 B.C., when Pericles accomplished the enfranchisement of the third class—the zeugitae[43]—by vote of the assembly. The poor thetes, constituting a substantial portion of the population, were permitted to vote on bills introduced in the assembly, but could not vote in the annual elections for the top officials. Pericles believed all citizens should be allowed the vote, so his organization circumvented the class system by allowing several thousand thetes to list themselves as zeugitae and thus enter their names on the voters' list. The mammoth irregularity was discovered in Pericles' absence and created a scandal.

Pericles' political lieutenant, who had engineered what the upper classes considered an election fraud, was a liberal teacher named Damon. Since Pericles' youth, Damon had been his teacher in the humanities. He became a rabid supporter of his student and was essentially the chairman of the Liberal Party. Plutarch described Pericles in his early years as "the young athlete of politics" and Damon as "his training master in those exercises."

The scandal gave the conservatives under Thucydides (not the historian) the chance to attack Pericles. While he was gone, they called a session of the assembly and, after bitter debate, Pericles' man, Damon, was banished from Attica for a term of ten years as a danger to the city.

The conservative party line is described by Plutarch in

---

[41]The pentacosiomedimnoi were the highest class of Athenians and had an income of 500 or more bushels per year. The pentacosiomedimnoi could be elected archons.

[42]The hippeis were Athenian knights or cavalry (literally "horsemen") with at least 300 bushels, who enlisted with their own horses.

[43]The zeugitae, the third class in the Solonian census, were the solid, middle property-class in Athens with 200 bushels, who served as heavily armed infantry soldiers; they are also known as hoplites.

his *Lives of the Noble Grecians and Romans*:

> . . . by him [Pericles] the common people were first encouraged and led on to such evils as appropriations of subject territory, allowances for attending theatres, payments for performing public duties, and by these bad habits were, under the influence of his public measures, changed from a sober, thrifty people, that maintained themselves by their own labors, to lovers of expense, intemperance, and license.[44]

The conservatives cried, in effect, that Pericles' political philosophy was to tax and tax, spend and spend, elect and elect. The construction of the Temple to Athena was the prime example. It became the symbol of Pericles' profligacy that was allegedly destroying the character of the people. It became the focal point of the political campaign that followed pitting Thucydides against Pericles, and the fate of the Parthenon hinged on the result of the election.

Pericles was furious at the ostracism of his beloved teacher and closest friend. The upper-class leaders were equally furious with the Periclean taxes that were siphoning their surplus. The campaign became as bitter and personal as those in the early years of American democracy.

Aspasia became as deeply involved in the campaign as the candidate. She entertained constantly at home. Half the citizens of Athens must have walked through their house. Pericles surmised that as many of them came to see Aspasia as to see him. Many voters brought their wives or hetaerae. The women wanted to see what Aspasia wore, how she coiffured her hair, what makeup and perfume she used, how she cared for her hands and feet, what comments she made that they could quote, and what philosophy was fashionable. Pericles was an ex-general with a faded luster, but a beautiful woman was always a celebrity.

The campaign conducted by Thucydides' organization

---

[44]Plutarch, *Lives of the Noble Grecians and Romans*, 188.

heightened Aspasia's notoriety. Pericles knew his dignity and respectability had always been assets. People wanted to be in awe of their leaders, to pedestal them somewhere between earth and Olympus, and to endow them with a little superhumanity. Pericles knew the people had so endowed him in the days of his power and he had cultivated it.

Besides the scandal of the registration lists, Pericles' opponents had another oar to row with. They had Aspasia. She, Thucydides decided, was the real hole in his armor. At plays and festivals when Aspasia appeared, some would shout, "Deianeira, Deianeira." They were unidentifiable demon voices vomiting out of a crowd. Deianeira had been one of the wives of Heracles (Hercules). Out of jealousy she had given him a robe that was supposed to keep him faithful to her. She had unwittingly accepted it from one who hated Heracles. When he put it on, it filled him with such excruciating pain that it killed him. The implication was that Aspasia was killing Pericles.

A salacious story was spread by the enemy. It was, in substance, that the gods were outraged by the fact that squill-headed Pericles' hetaera, Aspasia, was a common whorehouse operator in Megara before coming to Athens. She took daughters of citizens and freedmen and made harlots of them and became rich. Now she assisted Pericles in his degeneracy. When she was not in his bed herself, she provided him with wives and daughters of freedmen.

More reprehensible, it alleged, was the fact that Pericles used the building of the Temple of Athena for his own lecherous purposes. Phidias, Pericles' sculptor, had a shack on the Acropolis, which he ostensibly used as an office. There he lured models to pose for the frieze[45] of the temple. Actually, they said, the modeling was a deception. Phidias was

---

[45]The frieze was the part of an entablature between the architrave and the cornice. See the illustration on p. 153.

providing Pericles with hetaerae at the city's expense.

At the palaestra, they were saying that Pericles was sleeping with the wife of his young lieutenant, Mennipus. Pericles gasped and shook his head. He got credit for so much more pleasure than he experienced. His friends asked him if he had expected freedom of expression to go that far. He had become the victim of his own free speech philosophy. Must unbridled dissemination of lies be allowed?

He knew of no halfway point between complete gagging and complete freedom. The laws of slander and libel had not yet been conceived. But, if Pericles were reelected, he vowed Thucydides would regret the nature of his campaign.

He began to suffer from a corrosive animosity toward his enemy. Anaxagoras, his other great teacher, had taught him the debilitating power of anger and hatred. They could so warp a man's thinking as to make a mental eunuch of him. Regardless of the virulence of the provocation, the prudent man controlled his emotions rather than surrendering to them. If Pericles struck a citizen or permitted any of his staff to do so, it would be fatal to his political fortunes. He would have to hold up the shield of his serenity and allow the arrows to bounce off. He had to appear superior and aloof. Isolated events on a smaller scale in sixteen previous campaigns had confirmed Anaxagoras' teachings. He must not permit an enemy to grasp a loose thread in the fabric of his dignity. Once the cloth commenced to unravel, it would be completely destroyed.

He could wait. His time would come. For what Thucydides had said about Aspasia, he resolved to destroy him. His acrimony grew; his hatred swelled. All he could do was increase his power of self-control commensurate with the expanding intensity of his anger. It whipped him to feverish campaign activity.

The people loved picnics and shows. Citizens were invited to his farm and served food while jugglers manipulated balls and flute girls danced, and Sophocles, busy writing a play called *Antigone*, advanced Pericles' candidacy by singing poetry that glorified Athens.

Whenever he gave a picnic, people thronged for the food and entertainment, as well as a chance to hear the former general give fiery speeches attacking his competitor as a stooge of the rich, an agent of the oligarchs interested only in preserving their property and caring nothing about the plight of the poor. Pericles promised them steady jobs, prosperity promoted by public works, land in foreign countries for those dissatisfied with their lots in Attica, summer naval training with romantic world travel for those unable to find satisfactory work otherwise. The real issue was the choice between an economy managed by the government and one operated by the propertied class—government by politicians vs. government by the rich.

Thucydides shouted to the citizens gathered at the agora that Pericles was bribing the voters with promises he could not perform. In the palaestra where the propertied assembled, he charged Pericles with turning the government over to the thetes, who were the least educated and the least qualified, but the most numerous class. The intelligent, responsible minority would be ruled by the ignorant, irresponsible majority.

Thucydides probably used an attack designed to counter Pericles' appeal to the masses. He probably charged Pericles with angering the gods. Pericles' closest friends and advisors had been the atheists Damon and Anaxagoras. Pericles had engineered the escape of the impious scientist criminal. It was a desecration of the sacred Acropolis to turn over the building of temples to an atheist. Athena would never live in a home constructed by a hypocrite, who built only to buy votes and to glorify his own name.

Pericles, he charged, was setting the ambitious harlot, Aspasia, up to replace divine Athena as the queen of Athens.

Pericles' so-called temple of Athena would become the temple of Aspasia and would surpass the sanctuary of Aphrodite at Corinth as a house of harlotry. Pericles' impiety would cause Athena to withdraw her protection from the city.

Demeter would not live in the Telesterion of Eleusis, which was to be constructed by an unbeliever who had insulted her by refusing to be initiated into the Eleusinian mysteries. And, if the people of Athens turned their city over to the infidel, Pericles, she would cease to make things grow in Attica.

It was well-known that Pericles was not a respecter of Apollo's oracle of Delphi. In his sixteen years as general, not once had he consulted the oracle for advice, even when the gravest decisions waited on him. Only a fool would consider himself wise enough to govern a state without the aid of Apollo.

Many years before, Pericles had taken sides with the impious Aeschylus against Zeus, and with all his spending, he had failed to devote one obol to the completion of the temple of Zeus, which was started many years before. The gods would not be insulted forever. A day of reckoning was coming for Athens. If she did not repent, Zeus would aim his thunderbolts to destroy a god-forsaking city.

The campaign was the most bitter in the history of Athens. The freedom of speech Pericles had fostered permitted it to be so. Even as violently as Themistocles and Aristides had hated each other, never had their personal attacks been as vitriolic as this.

On the day of the election long lines of citizens would climb up the path to the summit of the Pynx where they would meet in assembly and scratch the names of their favorites on potsherds and drop them into an urn. When the archons closed the lids at sunset, Pericles knew that more votes had been cast than ever before in an Athenian election, in spite of the fact that five thousand names had been purged from the lists two years before. No one had made an accurate count, but the population of Attica, including Athens and all its suburbs, amounted to 400,000, of whom about 30,000 were metics, about 120,000 were slaves, and about 170,000 comprised the male citizens, their wives, and children. There would be some 45,000 men eligible to vote. Each citizen could vote for ten generals. There was a list supported by the oligarchs lead by Thucydides, and one proposed by the Liberal Party with Pericles' name at the top.

The archons took a day to count the votes, and the result was written in huge letters on a large sheet of papyrus and posted on the notice wall in front of the council house under the statues of the eponymous heroes. Pericles' aides copied the totals and raced to his house with the result. More citizens had voted for him than for any other candidate, and the majority elected were of his party. The election of 443 B.C. was a decisive victory for Pericles.

Pericles was chosen Chief General and returned to his office in the strategeion. Thucydides, though receiving far fewer votes than Pericles, was elected one of the ten and was relegated to a smaller office. Aspasia became queen of Athens again, honored and adored by the malleable majority. Pericles immediately proceeded to work on his first promise to himself: to complete the temple. He had the flag run up on the Pynx to signal a special session. It was primarily for this he had returned from the idyllic irresponsibility of leisure and travel to politics and the onerous duties of general. If he had failed to persuade the assembly to authorize his proposed construction appropriation, he would have considered retiring permanently.

It was a cool day, but the seats on the Pynx were filled. The rough woolen and leather cloaks and mantles of the thetes and zeugitae outnumbered the linens of the affluent.

The bill setting forth Pericles' proposed appropriations included a restoration of the pre-Thucydidean budget for the temple and the odeum.[46] The appropriation bill also included money for the design of a smaller temple on the Acropolis to be called the Erechtheum, dedicated to Athena and Poseidon on the spot where the olive-wood image of Athena Polias stood. It would provide a new home for the olive tree that legend credited to Athena and for the spring unearthed by the trident of Poseidon.

As soon as the clerk read the bill, Thucydides donned the crown of myrtle and stood before the rows of citizens perched on the wooden benches. In the cool early morning sun, his breath emitted words wrapped in white puffs of air. He was well-prepared and deliberate and his arguments marched like a cavalry of oxen, ponderous but powerful. We do not have his exact words, but we know the substance of his arguments. According to him, Pericles' proposals were the evil song of a siren, inducing Athenians to abandon the ship of democracy. They placed into the hands of one man the power to buy any Athenian election.

The son of a wrestler father, himself an unsuccessful Olympic contender, Thucydides weaved slightly before his audience as a wrestler, tempting his opponent to give him an opening. In the past, he argued, tyrants or kings had wielded dictatorial power over a polis by controlling its arms. Pericles had conceived a new, more subtle method—by controlling its treasury. The man who held the keys to the city's treasury held the destinies of its citizens in his hands as surely as a king who commanded an army. Pericles, he said, sought enough money to provide work for more than six thousand men for a year. That would buy enough votes to win any Athenian election.

The second reason, Thucydides contended, that the appropriation bill should be defeated was that it would be disastrous to the characters of the citizens. They would

---

[46]An odeum is a small, covered theatre.

grow to rely on the city and its leaders for their very food, clothing, and shelter instead of relying on themselves.

Finally, he proclaimed, Pericles' immoral use of the funds of the allies, without their approval, would destroy the league, create enemies of friends, and leave Athens alone to fight new enemies as well as the old. Athens could not hope to defend itself against renewed warfare by Persia or Sparta without the allies, and Pericles' plans would drive them away. Athens had already been criticized abroad for removing the common treasury of the league from the isle of Delos into Athens. Pericles' excuse had been to make it safe from the barbarians. But now the question they asked was, who will make it safe from Athens? According to Plutarch, Thucydides went on to shout:

> Greece cannot but resent it as an insufferable affront, and consider herself to be tyrannized over openly, when she sees the treasure, which was contributed by her upon a necessity for the war, wantonly lavished out by us upon our city, to gild her all over, and to adorn and set her forth, as it were some vain woman, hung round with precious stones and figures and temples, which cost a world of money.[47]

If Thucydides believed that Athens took that money or any part of it and used it to adorn this city with temples, music halls, and shrines dedicated to the glory of Pericles or some other politician, Athenians would not only be callously immoral but naively stupid, for the allies would cease paying dues and forsake the league.

As Pericles listened carefully to Thucydides' presentation, he became disturbed by the realization that his adversary was not merely a tool of the more-propertied classes but was sincere in the convictions he expressed. He was more dedicated to political principle than Cimon had ever been and for that reason, perhaps, a more effective opponent.

---

[47]Plutarch, op. cit., 191.

Thucydides' genuineness only made him a greater menace to the welfare of the majority of Athens' citizens. It intensified Pericles' determination to destroy him.

The fear he routinely suffered while waiting to speak was absent today. The compulsion to stand, interrupt Thucydides, and attack his arguments was so strong that Pericles could hardly restrain himself. He was tight as a drawn bow.

Finally, after what seemed hours, Thucydides concluded his laborious pounding and handed the wreath of myrtle to the clerk. Pericles was so eager to launch his attack that the clerk had to touch his arm and stop him until the myrtle had been placed on his head. The clerk apparently entertained some aesthetic pride about the placement of the crown, and Pericles chafed as the man painstakingly adjusted and readjusted it as though he were a jeweler fitting a woman with a tiara. When, finally, properly attired, he faced his audience, he had to tug on his own reins to keep from talking too fast. Again, history has not preserved the precise words, but we know what the substance was.

The first fact to be understood, Pericles pointed out, was that the bill contemplated the use of only a small part of the contribution of each ally. The overwhelming percentage of the money was to be Athens' own. Those citizens, represented by Thucydides who would have Athens account to the allies for every obol they contributed to the common treasury, should analyze the facts more carefully. If Athens should have written down for the allies every obol and the manner of its expenditure, then Athens also should have written down the name and manner of the dying of every Athenian who had fought and died for them. For the past ten years the allies had contributed only money and a few ships, while Athens had contributed much more money and most of the men.

Perhaps on the ledger beside each Naxos or Aegineton obol spent by Athens, they should place the name of an

Athenian citizen who died. For every drachma of Miletus money spent in Egypt, it cost an Athenian life. With every Thasos drachma spent in Cyprus, an Athenian chair was made empty. For every Rhodes or Chios obol spent in Cilicia or Phoenicia, an Athenian wife's or mother's heart was broken. For every Lesbian, Troizon, or Megaran drachma spent in Tanagra or Euboia or Coronia, Athens buried an Athenian father's son or a son's father.

His audience was mesmerized; their attention was so alive and intense that it was almost participation. But they had listened to Thucydides the same dedicated way. He prayed his power would hold, and their interest remain steadfast, for it seemed to him his life depended on the success of this speech. He knew Thucydides' arguments had sounded so logical, so devastatingly sensible, and so coldly sound. Perhaps his enemy had already taken possession of their minds, closed them, and locked the door. Pericles was determined to win, possess, and actuate them, even if he had to do it by the sheer strength of his own will.

He reminded them that their fathers had saved these same allies from slavery at Marathon, Salamis, and Plataea. And those in his audience had fought beside him, to save them from Persia and Sparta in this generation. The contribution in drachmae they sent, once received, was not theirs that gave it, but theirs that received it, as long as the receivers performed the conditions upon which they received it, i.e., the defense of the allies. Athens was amply prepared for successful war anywhere, anytime, and against anyone. That was the job for which it was paid. Athens was fulfilling its obligations to its allies and could continue to do so and still have a surplus in the treasury.

What then should they do with the surplus? Let it sit and mold, or should it be used to improve the city and give prosperity to its citizens? What more wise or noble project could be undertaken than to glorify Athena, the goddess worshiped by all Greeks, and at the same time provide work for the citizens of her city. Athena was not only Athens' goddess but a goddess also of her allies. Greeks from all over the world came to kneel at her altar at the time of the Panathenaea. Why should they not make a small contribution to help supply an altar on which they could kneel?

Citizens of allied cities came to the festival of Dionysia to enjoy Sophocles direct a play or a choir. Why should not they make a small contribution to the construction of the music hall?

Athens, he pointed out, was the cynosure of all Greek minds that would learn. It was the teacher of Greece, the heart of the body of the Hellas, the hub of its wheel. Allies looked to Athens not only for defense but for learning and pleasure and for the justice of its courts. Athens' juries adjudicated the commercial disputes of half the world. Athens paid thousands of drachmae to hundreds of Athenians who operated the legal machinery which helped protect the property and liberty of all Greeks. Athens had done even more than that for its allies. It had given them the pattern and, in some instances, actually set up the machinery for democracy in their cities.

The allies did not object to paying for the olives, pottery, silver, or marble they bought from Athens. Was it unfair, was it immoral for them to compensate Athens modestly for the greatest exports they acquired from Athens —justice and liberty? He would go on to a more practical line of argument. Idealism was a great motivator, but hunger was greater.

He may have asked them not to turn and look at the agora. It would only fill them with sadness. They would see men standing in lines waiting for bread, when they wanted to stand waiting compensation for an honest day's work. Athens spent thousands of drachmae every year sending citizens to sea to practice the arts of war. Thucydides did not claim *that* would ruin their characters. He did not say *that* would make slaves of them. He did not say placing *those* thousands on the city payroll would make the Chief General dictator of Athens. If paying men to practice the arts of war would not undermine their characters or destroy their freedom or make their paymaster a tyrant, then paying them to perform the arts of peace would not do so.

Athens paid marines to destroy. Why should it not pay masons to build? Athens could build structures that would bring it eternal honor and glory and while doing so give employment in all the arts and trades. To do the job the city would need all Athenians to the extent they could serve —smiths, carpenters, molders, founders, braziers, stone-cutters, dyers, ivory workers, painters, embroiderers, turners, merchants, mariners, shipmasters, cartwrights, wagoners, rope-makers, and miners. All of them in some way or other would prosper from this glorification of the gods and sublime service to Athens and to Greeks of all lands. The prosperity of Athens today and her immortality tomorrow depended on a vote *for* this appropriation. He urged them not to fail the gods or their fellow citizens.

He handed the myrtle to the clerk and sat down, unable to tell whether the silence of the citizens indicated agreement or rejection. He had done his best. He had never put more energy into a speech, more heart into his voice. To maintain his outward serenity, he tried not to think about how important the vote was to him. While he perspired in the cold, the president put the bill to a voice vote. The shouts in favor of its passage were so overwhelming that the call for the negative was a formality and the response feeble.

The acrimony of Thucydides' speech and the decisiveness of Pericles' victory convinced Pericles that now was the time to destroy the enemy who had vilified him and his wife and imperiled Athens. When the citizens returned to their seats after the morning meal, he counted the rows and the number in a row and estimated that there were more than six thousand present—the quorum necessary for what he hoped to do. When the president reconvened the meeting, Pericles stood, was recognized, and shattered the cool autumn air with a chilling motion for the banishment of Thucydides. A quick collective inhalation froze the audience.

Damon had been the last, slightly over a year before; and he had been the first since Cimon, who had succumbed more than sixteen years earlier. During Pericles' entire sixteen years of generalship, he had never invoked the banishment procedure, nor had it been used by anyone under him. Though Ephialtes, with Pericles' help, had disposed of Cimon for a time by means of the ostrakon, Pericles since becoming general had, in principle, been opposed to it. He had believed that he could retain power, if he served well, without resorting to the ruthless ostrakon to eliminate competition. But Thucydides' unscrupulous tactics had changed his point of view. In the one year Thucydides had been general, he had banished Damon and tried to ostracize Andokides, in an effort to strangle all competition—shades of the Areopagus. Pericles knew Thucydides would continually chew at him like the hawk-mouthed hounds of Zeus, undermining every program that Pericles considered constructive.

Pericles could forgive what Thucydides had done to him personally, but he would not forgive the banishment of Damon, the prosecution of Anaxagoras, and the abuse of Aspasia. Such a defiler of the innocent and persecutor of principle had no right to the blessings of Athenian citizenship.

The atmosphere that froze the citizens in their seats was not the autumn air. It was the memory of men recalling historic events: the ostracism of Pericles' uncle, Megacles; his father, Xanthippus; the now almost legendary Aristides and Themistocles; and the colorful and controversial Cimon. All momentous monuments to the violence of men's principles and passions. The president suspended the agenda, and

Pericles heard his voice penetrate a silence even deeper than the response to the morning debates.

Pericles firmly announced that the character and caliber of a man is exposed in a political campaign not by the tactics of his opponent but by the nature of his own methods. In a recent campaign and in the speeches this morning, this man, in the service of a few, dedicated to the subjugation of the many, had not only accused Pericles of being an atheist, an enemy of the gods, but he charged him and his friends with the most heinous personal acts of moral depravity. Worst of all, he had attempted to defile the name and reputation of Pericles' wife.

If Athenians who wished to serve their city must endure vilification of that nature in order to aspire to high office, soon there would be no one willing to aspire. Government by the many would succumb to government by the few who were so evilly, unconscionably ambitious as to resort to such improper methods. Such a man, he charged, evidenced all the tyranny of a Peisistratus and the monarchial madness of a Xerxes. Such a man would shorten Athens' breadlines only by taking away the bread. For the safety of Athens, for the security of democracy, for the rights of the individual Athenian citizen, Thucydides must be banished. Never had Pericles spoken in the heat of such hatred, but he had made it his servant. He had controlled it, and it had illuminated his mind, sharpened his tongue, and magnified the forcefulness of his appeal.

Thucydides, obviously shaken with surprise and fury, stood and floundered in his own defense. Never naturally fluent, his unorganized words stumbled out and fell over each other. He knew not whether to deny, explain, or attack. And, after struggling to regain his poise, he concluded by saying that he needed no defense and would submit himself to the fairness of his fellow citizens.

The clerks passed the earthen shards up the aisles. As

the assemblymen gravely filed by the urns and deposited the ostraka, they were grim and they did not look at Thucydides. Pericles watched his enemy as the result was read. Ten years seemed to have been added to the age of Thucydides' face by the time the clerk's voice ceased.

11

The Construction of the Parthenon

Naturally, the most famous hill of Athens is the Acropolis. On its summit, safe from marauding invaders, the first citizens of Attica gathered and built a tiny settlement. Legend informs us that Athena and Poseidon appeared before the inhabitants seeking to be adopted as the god or goddess of the city. Even in this dim prehistoric mural of the past, Athenians believed in the ballot and they decided to vote to select their ruling divinity. Each made a campaign pitch. Poseidon demonstrated his prowess by thrusting his trident into the rocky surface and producing a flowing spring of water. Athena struck the ground with her spear and an olive tree sprang forth full grown and weighted with olives, just as Athena herself had sprung from the head of her father, Zeus, full grown and fully armed.

Men and women voted. Athena won and it is said women were never permitted to vote again in Athens until 1937. No matter, the city was named Athena.[48]

On the Acropolis, meaning high city, there exist today four ancient ruins, beautifully preserved: the Erechtheum, a temple to Poseidon and Athena; the Temple to Athena Nike, an Ionic[49] jewel; the Propylaea, which is the magnificent, pillared stairway-entrance to the Acropolis; and the renowned Temple to Athena, which we know as the Parthenon. All were constructed as units of Pericles' public works project and completed in the fifth century B.C. The political backdrop to the construction of the world's most famous building, the Parthenon, is a drama worthy of the stylus of a Greek tragedian. Athens had been warring off and on with Persia for half a century. In 450 B.C., a treaty was signed between Athens and Persia and between Athens and Sparta.

Peace settled on Athens like a plague, and Pericles was in trouble. The agora, from the painted stoa on the north to the court house on the south, was bisected with bread lines of hungry men in ugly moods. For the last ten years thousands of people seeking freedom and fortune had come to the city from Greek and non-Greek lands. A law passed in 452 B.C. denying them citizenship, even if they married Athenian women, had not deterred them. People still migrated to the land of freedom. The statue of Athena Promachos, sculpted by Phidias in the 460s, visible from the gulf

---

[48]Its name today is Athena, though speakers of English call it Athens as a result of the modifications in passing from Greek to English.

[49]Ionic refers to the ancient Greek architectural order distinguished especially by columns on bases and scroll volutes in its capitals. The Doric order is distinguished by columns with no base and the channelings of the column are usually twenty in number. The Ionic is lighter and more graceful than Doric, while the Doric is older and simpler than Ionic. To understand the Greek architectural terms in this chapter, see the illustration on p. 153.

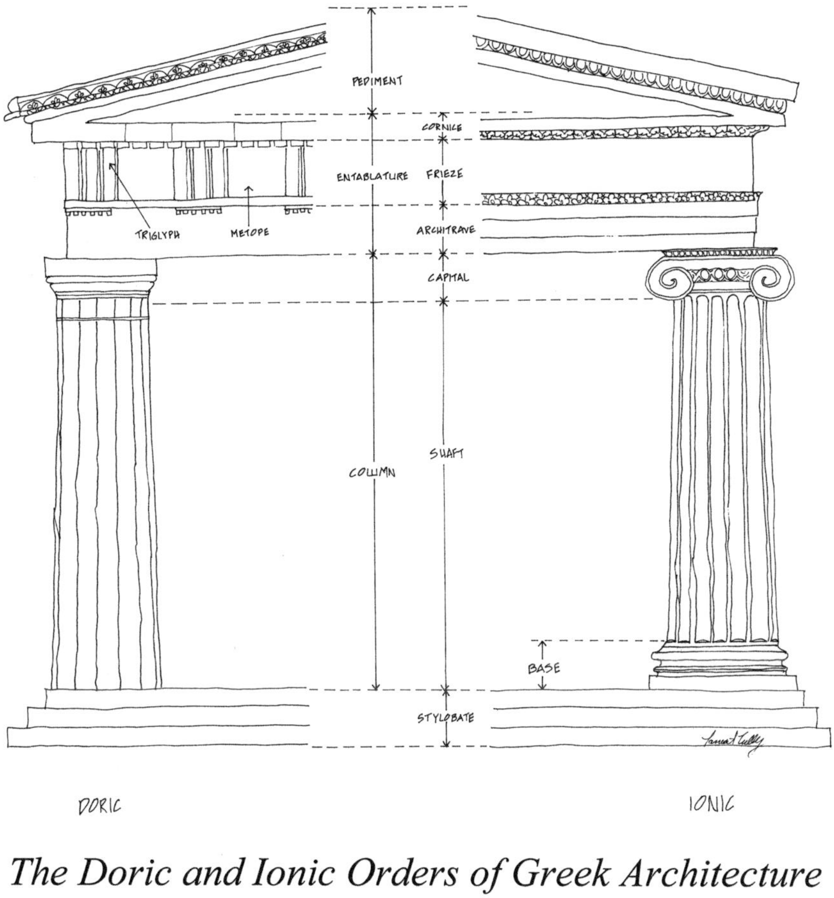

The Doric and Ionic Orders of Greek Architecture

as they approached Piraeus, like the Statue of Liberty in New York harbor centuries later, welcomed the tired and oppressed of every nation. For forty-two years, ever since Marathon, war had been one of the main industries in Athens. The peace treaties with Persia and Sparta eliminated the summer work for about forty thousand men (twenty percent of the male population), including citizens, metics, freedmen, and slaves—except eight thousand assigned to summer training. Yet, the city was rich if you measured its wealth by its treasury. The silver mines were still producing abundantly as they had in the time of Themistocles. But there were thousands of unemployed. Pericles, following the precedent established by Themistocles, did not simply divide up the silver production among the citizens. It went into the city treasury. Ever since the edicts of the wise Solon, Athenians had believed that men should work. They should produce. If a man did not produce, he was not a good citizen. He had to contribute his part to the wealth of the community. Standing in bread-lines was not Athenian. It was a disgrace to the descendants of the heroes of Marathon and Salamis. But the thousands of immigrants who had been invited since Cleisthenes, plus the men who had left the oars of the triremes, could not be absorbed on the farms or in the factories.

It was a significant moment when Pericles sent a runner to Olympia to beseech Phidias to come back to Athens as soon as he could complete the statue of Zeus he was executing there. Pericles was going to start a public works program and he wanted Phidias to direct it.

With Anaxagoras and Damon, Phidias was one of the three men closest to Pericles. They were the same age and probably had been companions since childhood, though the sculptor was the son of a humble painter and Pericles was the son of a general. Phidias had literally, and almost alone, changed the status of the sculptor from something akin to a carpenter to something resembling a playwright. When

General Cimon had seen some of the young man's work, he had the perceptiveness to applaud it. The realism of the statues was fantastic. His busts actually looked like men and women. There was expression in their faces and action in their bodies. Cimon probably commissioned him to do a bust of himself, and he had him do reproductions of his illustrious father, Miltiades. When Cimon looked at his likeness, he was amazed. It did not look simply like a noble general in the abstract—it looked like Cimon. Like his oligarchic predecessor, Peisistratus, Cimon had an appreciation for art and he had put Phidias to work for the city. As a very young man, Phidias had sculpted twelve life-sized statues of Athenian heroes which were erected at Delphi. Worshipers from all over the world had seen them and marveled, and Phidias was a panhellenic subject of admiration by the time he was thirty. Pilgrims may not have known the name of the talented Sicilian sculptor who had executed the superb charioteer, also gracing the precincts of Delphi, but they knew the name of Phidias.

The seventy-foot statue of Athena the Protector on the Acropolis in Athens embellished his fame. When relatives came from Rhodes to visit, it was one of the first things they were taken to see. Of course, they had already seen it from the harbor, but close up, on the base, they read, in small letters, the name "Phidias," and they marveled at his incredible ability to put life into bronze. He had turned a craft into an art. The people of the loyal island of Lemnos had commissioned him to place something on the Acropolis that would remind Pericles and the assembly that they were devoted to mother Athens. And he had sculpted a beautiful Athena of Lemnos which had put Athena in a chiton, made a beautiful woman of her instead of representing her as she usually appeared, a female warrior dressed in helmet and breastplate. The women adored Phidias for that. For the temple of Demeter in Eleusis, in Pericles' time, he had executed in eternal stone a moving depiction of Demeter and Persephone teaching Triptolemus, a mortal, how to plant grain. What the celebrated Sophocles had done in 468 B.C. in his first prize-winning play, *Triptolemus*, Phidias had done in stone—telling the story of how the gods gave the staff of life, the "marrow of men," to the Greeks.

Phidias had been asked to come to Olympia to fashion a statue of Zeus to be placed in the temple being built for the city of the games. The climax of all athletic tournaments was at Olympia and had been ever since 776 B.C. long before Solon made a significant city out of Athens. The temple was probably built by some panhellenic organization in which even Sparta and Athens cooperated. The fact that Phidias was asked to execute the personification of the god reveals that he was incontestably the leading sculptor of the Greek world.

We know little about Phidias' appearance or personality. He was probably a small man with big hands for he created great statues out of stone and bronze, but there is no evidence that he ever distinguished himself in war, whereas other outstanding Athenian artists—the best known is Sophocles—had become famous as generals. However, his statue of Zeus tells something about his personality and his appraisal of his art. While he was sculpting his statue, the contractors were building the temple. He, no doubt, had the plans and specifications in his possession, but they did not deter him. He had his idea as to what the representation of Zeus should be, and the architects of the temple be damned. When he finished his statue, it was all out of proportion with the size of the temple—much too large. So they altered the temple to accommodate it.

When Pausanius saw the temple six centuries later, he was much moved by the statue of Zeus. Viewing the statue of Zeus was a spiritual experience, according to him, and it was later classified as one of the seven wonders of the ancient world. Tragic it is that about A.D. 425 it was taken by the Turks to Istanbul and destroyed. Today its likeness appears only on Olympian coins.

It is understandable why Pericles asked this artistic genius to return to Athens at this time. He had a problem; all the artists, craftsmen, playwrights, poets, and painters were at his disposal. They knew he was the man who kept the political climate favorable, the world at peace, and the economy prosperous so they could work.

Pericles looked at it this way. Twenty-two years before, the Persians had leveled Athens' temples. Greece, not just Athens, should rebuild them. A letter had gone out not only to Athens' 180 allies but to all Greek cities, including Sparta. The letter called a meeting to discuss joint rebuilding of the temples destroyed by Persia. It was time to erect the symbols of victory and freedom from the domination of the tyrants of Asia. If the cities of the Hellas were to retain the ideals and the courage to remain unchained, they must have symbols to fight for. The memory of Marathon, Salamis, and Plataea was dimming. Many who had fought were now dead, and their grandchildren must have symbols of those triumphs over tyranny to inspire them.

Too many Athenians now did not know what freedom was because they had not known what slavery was. They did not feel its breath on their backs as Pericles' father had. They would not fight as his father had at Salamis and as he had fought at the Eurymedon and Tanagra because freedom was an abstract idea. But they would fight for Athena. To them she was real, and they could love her and fight and die for her or live and build for her. Pericles knew that the freedom they had in Athens was not a perennial flower—it was an annual. Any year they could lose it by invasion from without or ignorance and greed from within. The spirit of the people made the difference.

He wanted a temple to Athena. He wanted Phidias to supervise the entire construction of the building. He trusted him and, in addition, wanted him to sculpt a likeness of

Athena that would be the greatest work he had ever done.

Pericles had already engineered the construction of the Telesterion of Eleusis. This is an example of his political sensitivity, since thousands trekked to Eleusis every year to see the shining hieron and pay tribute to the Goddess Demeter. The hierophants, their leaders, influenced a lot of votes. For that task the hierophants and Pericles had selected the brilliant young Ictinus to be the architect, and he had done a superb job. Another architect, Callicrates, had drawn plans for a tiny temple, Athena Nike, to be built on the Acropolis, but the work had not yet commenced. Pericles decided to use both men to build a large temple to Athena at the center of the Acropolis where Cleisthenes had laid the foundations sixty years before.

Phidias returned from Olympia and barely had time to respond to thc toasts of his fellow citizens for his spectacular Zeus before Pericles had him surveying the site for the new temple. Ictinus and Callicrates were with them. They wandered the surface of the Acropolis wending their ways through the stubble of statues. As they encountered statues of Xanthippus and Themistocles, Pericles stopped a moment, and they stood in silence. Probably nearby workmen were putting in place a statue of the recently deceased Cimon. It is likely Cimon had expressed the desire that a statue of him be executed by another great sculptor, Phidias' chief competitor, Myron. In 450 B.C. Athenians had stood in awe and then cheered as Myron's statue of the discus thrower was unveiled on the Acropolis. Never had a sculptor caught such daring action in marble. Cimon would want the sculptor of action to do a statue of him. The other generals, knowing Cimon was to be depicted in action, probably took bets as to whether Myron would have him performing on the battlefield or in bed, since he had proven himself accomplished in both arenas. No doubt, the statue postured him holding his sword high, gesturing his troops forward. They stopped at the base of the towering statue of Athena Promachos. Pericles would observe that Phidias had been wise to face her to the west so she could keep an eye on Sparta.

It is believed that Ictinus was tall and thin with black, thoughtful eyes and an egotistic awareness of his own genius. Callicrates was husky, quick-moving, blunt-speaking, and loved to work with his hands as well as his mind. Ictinus, the dreamer; Callicrates, the driver; Ictinus, the designer; Callicrates, the builder—Pericles wanted that combination. He had used Callicrates to design and supervise the construction of the long wall to Piraeus. It was a rush job, and Callicrates organized the labor crews skillfully, worked them at a feverish pace, and finished the wall before the Spartans could do anything about stopping it.

Pericles looked with disapproval at the patched-up temple of Athena Polias on the north edge of the plateau and with annoyance at the altar of Zeus and the sanctuary of Artemis, both of which had been erected nearly a hundred years before by Peisistratus and had been repaired and partially re-erected after the ravages of the Persians. He believed the handiwork of a tyrant had no place on the Acropolis, but probably on the advice of Herodotus, he would not destroy them because of their historical value.

For more than ten years, Pericles' dream of a magnificently pillared structure on the highest point on the Acropolis had gradually taken form in his mind. Many of the column drums hauled there to be used in Cleisthenes' temple were still strewn over the Acropolis and perhaps could be used in the new temple along with the still extant foundation. They were of the type of marble Pericles wanted to use, the gold-cream flesh quarried from Mt. Pentelicus.

He had only a vague vision and did not try to set any specific design for fear it would blind him of the beauties of the plans of an Ictinus. But his vision had a spirit. He wanted a building austere enough to adorn Olympus, warm enough to grace a vineyard. He saw a regal mansion for a goddess that would be a part of the Acropolis and yet suspended in the sky—a structure combining heavenly and earthly architecture suitable in either sphere. He wanted a giant, anchored trireme, floating, able to weigh anchor and sail away. He envisioned many graceful columns and a solid inner structure to give seclusion to Athena's person and security to Athens' money. He saw the gods of the Greeks, the heroes of the Hellas, and the big and little people of Athens in a panathenaic profusion of sculptured marble adorning the temple.

Painstakingly, he conveyed his ideas to the architects and the sculptor. He told them he wanted the largest, and at the same time, the most beautiful building ever constructed in the Hellas. He did not want them to throw money away, but he wanted the best—regardless of cost.

Ictinus was already designing in his mind. If he could have unlimited funds, he could employ the subtleties required to produce the type of structure Pericles wanted. What were the subtleties, Pericles would want to know. Ictinus would say, you want the roof to look like it is weightless on the columns, but you want the columns to be graceful. That was exactly what Pericles wanted. The columns would be more than thirty feet tall. If they were of the same diameter all the way, they would appear to the eye to be smaller at the center and therefore fragile. The superstructure would appear to rest heavily on them—a matter of optics. The base diameter of the columns, if they used the same ones Cleisthenes had started with, would be six and a quarter feet. They would have to increase the diameter in a gradual, exactly specified swell about forty percent of the distance up the column, then taper in so the top diameter would be less than the bottom. That plumpness of the column was necessary to make it appear to be the same size all the way up and give it the desired appearance of strength and grace. This would require painstaking stone cutting. In addition to that, they would have to slant the columns inward slightly at a carefully computed angle to avoid an impression of sagging.

Also, the distance between the columns at the corners would need to be somewhat shorter for aesthetic reasons. Those were only a few of the subtleties that would cost hundreds of extra man-hours and thousands of drachmae.

No matter—Pericles wanted it built with all the subtleties. Let him worry about the money. He would wheedle the assembly into appropriating it. Nothing was too good for Athena. Then he confronted the architects with the impossible. He wanted it completed in ten years. They thought he was out of his mind. He reminded them they would not use slave labor. They would have well-paid workers—citizens, metics, freedmen, and slaves, all paid the same for the same work—equals on the job within their trades. They would see free men work the way free men fight.

Arrangements were made to house the guests Pericles expected from the other Greek cities to attend his temple-building conference. He was angry when some of the cities wrote that they would not be sending representatives. He received information that Sparta had sent agents to some and letters to all of the members of the Peloponnesian League opposing their attendance at the meeting. Nevertheless, Pericles expected more than one hundred delegates to come from the cities of the Athenian League. He prepared his speech carefully—and with love.

To his shock and disappointment, no one—not a single delegate—showed up for the meeting, except the Athenians who had been invited. With Anaxagorean equanimity he controlled his anger and spoke with the same enthusiasm to his own people that he had hoped to display to the representatives of the far-flung empire. He undoubtedly reminded them that it was not the first time Athens had done a job for the rest of Greece. Athens would build the temple alone.

On most days during the construction of the Parthenon, Pericles would hike up to the high city, the Acropolis, and watch the men work. The placement of each stone of golden marble gave him satisfaction. The hill was as busy and alive as a disturbed ant bed. It was the hub of a wheel that was turning with prosperous, happy activity. It was a pregnant woman, two years along now with an extraordinary child —the temple of Athena Parthenos—and she was more than beginning to show. The foundation, floor, and surrounding steps were completed.

He stood at one end of the floor and sighted along the slight convexity curving its length. The same convexity now would appear in the architrave[50] which rested on the columns. There would not be one absolute straight line in the whole structure. All lines would be slightly curved as were the lines of the human body, which was the basis of beauty. It would help give Pericles the trireme temple anchored to earth, floating in the sky. As he observed the artistry, he smiled and felt very knowledgeable.

Though Phidias was in charge of all construction, he devoted most of his time to sculpting the giant Athena. He was creating her, in place, on a newly laid floor of the great temple. She would stand forty feet tall. He would not repeat the mistake he made at Olympia, where he created a god too big for his temple. This temple would be big enough to house the goddess. Her body was being carved of stone. Then she would be covered with flesh of ivory and garments of gold. She would be the most costly and the greatest accomplishment in the history of sculpture. That was what Pericles believed Phidias could do; that was what he had asked for and offered to pay for; and that was what Phidias was confidently attempting to do. Pericles watched Callicrates move from one group of workmen to another, sometimes complimenting and sometimes criticizing. And Ictinus was inspecting every inch of the job.

Pericles walked to the east end of the Acropolis and

---

[50]The architrave was the lowest division of an entablature resting immediately on the capital of the column.

looked along the road that wound southeastward through the cluttered, white-stuccoed houses, out the wall gates, through the farms, and disappeared on the slopes of Mt. Pentelicus. The road had been surfaced with gravel so that heavy loads of marble could be hauled over it. Pericles could see a train of carts pulled by as many as twenty oxen or mules laboriously lugging the blocks toward the Acropolis.

He had gone with Phidias and the architects to the quarries at Mt. Pentelicus before they started cutting and selected the area from which they wanted the stone quarried. After the stones had been cut out and laid in the sun to dry and they had dried for many days and were ready for the mason, Pericles had returned and watched the master-dresser move from stone to stone and quickly but carefully discard those flawed, or too hard to cut or with too many holes, or unduly porous and vulnerable to decay. He kept only those which were solid and would cut truly. Then he marked them, assigning the heaviest for the base of the temple and the hardest for the architrave.

Pericles saw the strippers follow the master-dresser and go to work on the selected stones and strip them of the soft outer surface and abrase them with powdered marble to flatten their bearing sides.

They were inspected and sorted again by the dressers. And by means of ramps, hooks, slings, ropes, levers, and rollers they were loaded onto the carts and transported to the base of the Acropolis. There the skilled stonecutters went to work with their hammers and chisels and expertly carved the flesh of the mountain into blocks for the walls, slabs for the floors and ceilings, drums for the columns, and plates for the metopes.[51] The carpenters had constructed wooden ramps; the rope-makers had made strong ropes; and the unskilled

---

[51]A metope was the space or rectangular panel between the triglyphs in the Doric frieze, often being decorated with figures in relief.

labor ran the ropes through the holes in the centers of the drums, pulled them up the ramps onto the Acropolis, and lined them up ready for incorporation into the structure.

It thrilled Pericles to observe that, directly or indirectly, thousands of men participated in the building of the temple. It gave work to all trades. He walked out of the cella,[52] surveyed the plateau, and listened to the teeming activity. Hammers pounded, chisels chipped, adzes grooved, saws screeched, mules brayed, and oxen groaned.

He could hardly wait for the inner rooms to be completed and see the magnificent columns begin to rise. A dream in embryo is the song of the soul. As he hiked down the trail, he observed the crowded agora. At the south end near, the engaging world traveler and prolific writer, Herodotus, held an audience spellbound as he read a chapter of his *History*, which he had probably written the day before. Beyond Herodotus' enraptured audience, hundreds of people stormed the stoas purchasing everything, and scores circulated through the law courts and other government buildings.

As the workers continued their labor, the walls of the cella rose to the square. The ramps were built, and the segments for the columns cut, pulled up, and lifted onto the ascending columns. The architrave was laid lightly on the columns; the pediments[53] at each end were crowded with the awesome sculptured figures of Grecian gods. The resplendent roof, shingled with painted red tile, crowned the structure.

Even though a bitter war with Samos intervened in 439 B.C., the temple was completed by midsummer of the next

---

[52]A cella was the enclosed, inner room or body of a temple, as distinct from its porticoes and other external parts. In the Parthenon the cella contained the statue of Athena.

[53]A pediment was the triangular space that forms the gable of a low-pitched roof and which was usually filled with relief sculpture in Greek architecture.

year. It was unbelievable. The world's greatest temple had been constructed in nine years. It was ready for dedication as a climax to the celebration of the Greater Panathenaea, a quadrennial festival of games and artistic contests commemorating the birth of Athena, held on what our calendars would designate the first of July.

On the morning of the fifth and final day of the Greater Panathenaea, after the contests were all completed, Pericles and Aspasia sat on the parade reviewing stand. With them were their bright, eleven-year-old son, Pericles, the Younger, the dull-witted Cleinias, and the twenty-two-year-old Xanthippus. The other boys were in the parade. Thousands lined the Panathenaic Way from the Ceramicus, outside the city wall, where the parade assembled, southeastward through the gate, across the agora, and up the west slope of the hill. It was midsummer. The sun was hot and the dust hung in the air like a dry vapor. It gave early excuse for the quaffing of wine on the joyous birthday of the goddess.

Pericles caught sight of the flute players leading the parade when they rounded the Hill of Colonus and started to diagonal across the marketplace. The gay flutes filled the air with merry melodies. Tradition fancied that the impish Pan escaped the woods and wafted invisibly fore and aft above the boys, piping the parts for them to play.

The leading public officials of Athens proudly followed the musicians: the nine generals other than the Chief General, the nine archons, the ten treasurers of the Greeks, and the ten treasurers of the goddess. Some of them were old and walked slowly up the hill, and the mounted marshals paced the young players so they would not leave too great a gap between them and the city's governors.

Behind them marched the embassies from other Greek cities carrying gifts to Athena. Many men from many lands in multicolored raiment: Spartans in short, woolen tunics; Thracians in skins and patterned mantles; and Cretans in tunics with diamond designs. Pericles was probably advised over the pandemonium of marching music and cheering crowds that more than 150 foreign governments were represented in the parade.

Much of the cheering concentrated on the next segment—the winners of the games. The four previous days had been filled with athletic and artistic contests. First came the ten judges of the games, then the ten judges of the nonathletic contests. Euripides had been a judge of the poetry reading contest but would not walk in the parade. The first winners, walking abreast and flexing their superior muscles, were the boy, youth, and men winners in their respective divisions of the boxing, jumping, pancration,[54] pentathlon,[55] running, and wrestling contests.

Pericles would stand to observe his foster son, twelve-year-old Alcibiades, who had probably conquered all competitors in the boys' wrestling contest. Their talented son, Pericles, the Younger, could not enter the contests because he was not a citizen at this time.

Next strode the crew of the winning trireme of the regatta staged the previous day in the straits of Salamis. The broad-shouldered crew of the triumphant tribe promenaded proudly. The strutting steeds of the winners of the horse races and the chariot race clopped closely on the heels of the rowers. Particularly popular with the crowd, most of whom had seen the event, was the riding spearman, who had won the exciting contest of throwing a javelin at a stationary shield from a galloping horse.

Then came the celebrated champions of the nonathletic contests. The best reader of Homeric poetry marched mod-

---

[54]A pancration was an ancient Greek athletic contest involving both boxing and wrestling.

[55]A pentathlon was an athletic contest involving participation by each contestant in five different events.

estly, trying to ignore the applause. Pericles himself may have judged the oratorical contest. He had presented the oil-filled amphora[56] to a competitor as gifted in his field as the javelin thrower was in his.

Those contests, held in the odeum the first day of the festival, were followed on the second by the flute and lyre competition. The third day hosted the thrilling choirs. The lyre and flute winners carried their instruments and marched ahead of the fifty-voice choir of the winning tribe. There was a noticeable gap between the columns of the choir and the next contingent, which the marshals did not try too hard to close up. The next marchers were the veterans of Marathon and Salamis, Plataea, Sestus, and Mycale, and they placed themselves deliberately. They took a tug at Pericles' heart, for if his father were still alive he would be marching in the front line. Fifty-two years had battled by since Marathon. Gray hair glinted in the summer sun, and rusting shields shone bright.

Then came the veterans who were Pericles' contemporaries. His life filed by as he watched his comrades-in-arms. His eyes left the procession and he saw it again as it had been: fighting fear and Persians at the Eurymedon with Cimon waving him forward; the campaign in Macedonia; the fame of first command at Aegina; the fierce cavalry fighting and fatigue and futility at Tanagra; and last year, the rewarding battle against Samos to keep the league intact.

They were all there marching—those who lived and could march. Some marched only in his mind: Cimon, Ephialtes, Cleinias, Myronides, Leocrates, and Tolmides—all good generals, and all long gone. More than thirty years of war wearily walked by while he stood and saluted. A

[56]An amphora was an ancient Greek jar or vase with a large oval body, narrow cylindrical neck, and two handles that rose almost to the level of the mouth.

lump lined his throat.

The next group brightened his mood but provoked his sentiments still more. The ephebes were two thousand beardless, smartly stepping eighteen- and nineteen-year-olds; and his son Paralos was probably leading one of the ten crews. Paralos was hardly material to become a general, but he was a good marine and an affectionate son. As his son saluted him and he returned it sharply, the lump enlarged. He put his arm around Pericles, the Younger, who knew he would never march with the cadets. This was the one growing shadow that darkened Pericles' day.

Then came the virgins who half marched, half danced as they followed closely on the handsome ephebes and swung their baskets of banquet utensils to be used at the feast to come. They glowed in utter ecstacy, pressed between the ephebes in front and the barelegged, sixteen- and seventeen-year-old horsemen, whose Thessalian steeds pranced pompously behind them. One could detect the enhanced prosperity of Athens by the increased number of families able to buy a boy a horse. There were probably at least ten times as many horses in the parade now as there had been when Pericles was a boy.

Then came the star of the great play: the trireme on wheels with Athena's saffron robe, woven all year by chosen virgins, gracefully draped on the mast and halyards of the ship, and dramatically telling in tapestry the battle of Zeus and Athena against the giants. The cheers grew deafening as the float approached. Finally, bellowing, snorting, protesting, and plodding came the oxen for the feast, driven onward by the priests of Athena.

Pericles and Aspasia, followed by the reviewing party, left the stand and walked through a fissure in the milling multitude toward the gleaming temple. The sight of it enraptured Pericles, and he stopped and stared. It was midday and the sun, approving its affinity to the color of the marble, performed the opening ritual of the dedication by setting fire to the stone. The climbing columns were golden flames halted on their way to the sun, their home, by the floating crown of marble entablature[57] and radiant roof that lay like a lover on the incandescent shafts.

He did not want to move from this panoramic view, but he had to and forced himself to emerge from his sublime absorption by thinking of statistics that would interest his guests. Probably someone would want to learn that the temple was about 228 feet long and 104 feet wide; that its outside columns, seventeen on each side and eight on each end, were made of drums, slightly more than six feet in diameter at the base of the column and three feet high.

Perfect beauty was the perfect human form, according to Phidias. And the human form contained no straight lines. The subtle curves and slants of the building were related to the curves of an athlete's legs changing with the play of muscles as columns are altered by the play of light.

As Pericles looked along the northern entablature of the temple located between the Doric capitals of the columns and the cornice[58] of the roof, he saw the majestic sweep broken up into over thirty metopes, separate scenes that reviewed the epochal action of the Trojan war refought in marble, recreated by the magic hammers and chisels of Phidias and his assistants.

Pericles was stirred by the dramatic colors Polygnotus had dictated to decorate parts of the structure. The background of the Trojan scenes was the color of blood. The backgrounds of the pediments on each end of the building

---

[57]An entablature was the horizontal part in Greek architecture that rested upon the columns and consisted of architrave, frieze, and cornice.

[58]The cornice was the molded and projecting horizontal member that crowns an architectural composition.

were the hue of the Attican sky. The narrow triglyphs[59] that separated the metopic pictures were dark blue as were the cornices. The roof was tiled in resplendent red. The colors complemented the sky above, the hills around, and the sea beyond. But the steps, floor, columns, and architrave remained unpainted, and the marble's golden, glazen translucency dominated the design.

The chisel of Phidias had merged with the stylus of Ictinus and the paint of Polygnotus to give Pericles his dream: a building austere enough to adorn Olympus and warm enough to grace a vineyard—a regal mansion for a goddess that was part of the Acropolis yet suspended in the sky—a giant, anchored trireme, floating, able to weigh anchor and sail. The genius of the sculptor and architects, implemented by the skill of the artisans and the expenditure of more money than had ever been spent on a building, had created what Hippodamus declared was the most soul-lifting structure in the world.

The rolling, robe-adorned trireme had been pulled to a stop in front of the east entrance to the temple. Pericles and his reviewing-stand guests proceeded to the trireme, turned, and faced the temple. As a priest with a long knife skillfully killed the oxen for the sacrificial offering, Pericles looked up at Phidias' panoply of sculpture on the east pediment of the temple depicting the birth of Athena from the head of Zeus, as the astonished family of gods stared. There the impermanence of man became the permanence of gods, the mortal became immortal, the weak strong, the mundane sublime, and the sordid sacred. The thousands, Athenian and non-Athenian, who thronged the rock would come and go, but generation after generation, century after century they would stand where Pericles stood now and look up and see the pro-

---

[59]A triglyph was a feature of the Doric frieze, consisting of a slightly projecting rectangular tablet separating the metopes.

duction of one mind by another; the genesis of truth, of wisdom, the first triumph of mind over matter, of brain over body; the symbol of the ever-evolving reproducibility of knowledge and reason—Athena, magically materialized from the mind of Zeus.

Hephaestus stood behind them, stunned, with the ax limp in his hands with which he had struck his father's head and launched truth into eternity. The gods, assembled on the sides in wonder, watched the miracle unfold.

For months Pericles had observed the dedicated Phidias, working on this pediment from the sun's first light at dawn until its last red rays burned cold at night. Then the sculptor, exhausted, would go inside and lie by the feet of the mighty mistress he had created. Through puffs of marble dust, Pericles had seen the lifeless slab of stone of the pediment become a womb and then a multi-embryo. Lines grew into legs, figures into faces, chips into clothes, and scratches into swords; then muscles grew on limbs, expressions entered eyes, awe fixed itself on open mouths, breasts admitted animation, and life reached out through arms to finger ends. A multitude of mighty gods stood still by the hand of man.

When the smoke of sacrifice had wafted up and given the assembled gods a whiff of earth's ambrosia, beef, and the winning choir had sung, Pericles led a selected segment of the procession through the columns into the peristyle,[60] then through the giant doors into the consecrated cella. Close behind him in solemn cavalcade were those who carried, with the care of body bearers, the massive yellow peplos cut to fit a thirty-six-foot goddess.

From the blazing outside sun, they moved to the tender torchlight of the interior. The torches were aided by slender shafts of sunlight which invaded through narrow apertures of

---

[60]A peristyle was a colonnade surrounding either a building or an open space.

the ceiling and continually altered their angles. Shifting lights and shadows gave animation to the goddess and the inside columns that attended her. The fluid panorama gave life to lifeless forms.

Once inside, the procession waited while Pericles involuntarily stopped, stalled in his tracks by the breathtaking spectacle of the goddess, six times his height, who faced him from the end of the room. The ivory flesh of her bare hands, arms, face, and feet held the white softness of the inside of a child-bride's thigh. Her permanent peplos and chiton were molded of gold, and the flowing folds rippled as they reflected the flames and the slanting sunbeams.

In her right hand she held a gold-draped statue of a Nike,[61] which was the size of a tall young girl. Her left hand steadied a standing shield resting on the base. Her golden helmet shrouded tawny hair that flooded down below it. The Olympian Athena sprang from the head of Zeus, but she came to earth and in mortal birth she sprang from the hand of Phidias.

Pericles strode forward and stopped in front of the goddess as six excited, fire-lighted virgins, three on each side of the statue, climbed carefully up temporary ladders holding the robe with one hand and the rungs with the other. At the top of their ascent, they painstakingly slid the peplos over the helmet and slowly moved it beyond the face to the neck and let it cascade downward over the glistening gold. They buttoned it over the shoulder and straightened up on their ladders with tears in their eyes and ineradicable memories in their maiden hearts.

The procession stood silent while another sacrifice was consummated. Pericles relaxed and looked around the cella. The sturdy walls and brilliantly painted, coffered ceiling "trapped" the goddess safely from the blazing light, the salt

---

[61]Nike was the Greek goddess of victory.

wind from the sea, and the murmuring crowd outside. Inward a few feet from the walls saffron streams of marble fountained upward from the floor. The fluted columns climaxed in Doric capitals shouldering the floor of a balcony colonnade.[62] Then the columns seemed to thrust up through their capitals and flow on to the ceiling, thus providing pillars for the upper colonnade.

The priest signaled the conclusion of his sacrifice, and Pericles turned and led the procession over the smooth slabs of marble out again into the shining day. He sat on the stylobate[63] and surveyed the crowding multitude. It would not be an occasion for a long speech. Too many uncomfortably standing, too many children, too many straining, too far away, who could hear the sound of his words but not distinguish the words of his sounds. Too much wine had been drunk too early in the day. His speech would be brief. That made it more difficult. The occasion was so important, it was so hard to say what was sufficient to say when it had to be said concisely. He must speak the right words for metics as well as citizens, non-Athenians as well as Athenians, enemies as well as allies. This day was not only panathenaeic, it was panhellenic. He wanted his temple to be in the custody of Athens for the inspiration of all. He wanted all Greeks to come to Athens, make sacrifices to Athena, and identify her with Athens as Athens' defender. A not very subtle way of building a spiritual wall possessing military might to welcome men's hearts and repel their swords.

To Pericles, the temple and the statues were the enshrinement of truth, wisdom, and the rule of law. Most of his people were believers in the literal, corporeal reality of

---

[62]A colonnade was a series of columns set at regular intervals and usually supporting the base of a roof structure.

[63]A stylobate was a continuous base or platform upon which a row of columns was supported.

Athena. To them, perhaps the temple constituted an even more tangible spiritual substance. First, it would lift their spirits and deliver them a draught of what Socrates heralded as the aim of all—happiness. Second, it would give them a breast from which to suck security.

It was a legitimate bribe to Athena. She would live in the best home offered. This was it. She could not resist sitting in the cella and beaming over her beatific likeness or viewing the eastern pediment dramatizing her extraordinary birth, or exulting over the west pediment where Phidias had fashioned cosmic forces fighting for the earth: Athena's tree-planting triumph over Poseidon and her glorious acquisition of Attica. Her presence was protection.

Pericles cared little with what degree of superstition or sophistication his people worshiped her. At any level it was wholesome for them and for Athens—as long as Athena stood for the things Pericles stood for. For himself, he worshiped this Athenian sanctuary of supremacy because it helped make and maintain Athens as the hub of the wheel, the heart of the Hellas, and the school of the Greeks.

12

The Echoing Voices

Following the dedication of the temple, Pericles and Aspasia held a reception at their home on a hill overlooking the agora for their friends and those who had contributed most to the completion of the magnificent project. Their gardened courtyard would be illuminated by flaming torches. Extra chairs and couches would be placed to accommodate the guests.

Pericles probably wore a gold-bordered tunic and a purple himation[64] draped formally but comfortably over the left side of his chest and his left shoulder, leaving his right arm free. While dressing, he could take note of the fact that at fifty-four his abdomen was still flat and hard, but half of the hair on his chest, as on his head, had turned gray. Aspasia,

---

[64]A himation was a rectangular cloth draped over the left shoulder and about the body and worn as a garment in ancient Greece.

at thirty-two, was probably as beautiful to Pericles as she had been at twenty, when he first took her to his home. Her white linen chiton would hang in folds to her ankles and her blue himation, wrapped tightly around her, erotically etched the curves of her body and left both arms bare except the lower left, which supported one end of the garment.

Her golden hair, disciplined by a jeweled tiara, flowed down like a fountain of honey to the tips of her beautifully sculptured shoulders. Her eyes flashed jade, and he could not tell whether the green jewels of her tiara were reflected in her eyes or her eyes gave luster to the jewels.

One of the first arrivals would be Socrates, son of Sophroniscus. Most of Pericles' information about him had come from Aspasia. Anaxagoras, Pericles' beloved teacher, may have introduced his student, Socrates, to her, and for years Socrates, slightly younger than Aspasia, had been one of her students of rhetoric and one of her most ardent admirers. He was odd in appearance and unkempt in his habits. He was the son of a humble, undistinguished stone-cutter and a distinguished midwife who may have delivered Pericles' children. Socrates at this time was thirty-one, the age at which Pericles had become a general. Pericles had met him fleetingly when he had been at the house as a teacher of his sons or a student of his wife. The young man's independence, ease, and naturalness and the glint of humor in his eyes somewhat compensated for his shabby dress and indolent manner. His homeliness was arresting and Pericles would take a double and sympathetic look at him, because nature had been as cavalier with the sculpturing of Socrates' face as it had been with Pericles' longish head. However, apparently little rapport had developed between the unorthodox young teacher-philosopher and the general. Pericles was a busy and preoccupied man. Moreover, Socrates had never exhibited much interest in or deference toward the powerful Pericles. Pericles was part of establishment and Socrates, to his death, was in a constant quarrel with the establishment.

Pericles may have had serious doubts about Socrates' merits as a teacher, for he certainly had been unable to make a man out of his recalcitrant son, Xanthippus.

Socrates' father had taught him the trade of stone mason and sculptor, and occasionally he worked at it but had spent most of his time studying with teachers and conversing and teaching at the agora on the steps of the Stoa of Zeus. He accepted students informally in large or small groups, charging them nothing. He had a small income from his father's estate and seemed not to care about material things. He supplemented his meager income occasionally by accepting compensation from rich citizens who sought his services. Aspasia had, no doubt, compensated him generously for teaching their children. She did not charge him for rhetoric lessons because he reciprocated by teaching her philosophy. Socrates would not dress up for this auspicious occasion. He would wear his usual frayed tunic. He was not as tall as Pericles, but was as powerfully built as an Olympic wrestler; his head was big, his face broad, his nose wide and snubbed with flared nostrils, his lips thick, his forehead high, his beard heavy, and his hair untrimmed. He looked more like fifty than thirty except for his large eyes, which were alive, expressive, and amused with life.

Pericles was inclined to overlook Socrates' indifference to the Chief General of Athens because of General Andokides' report of him. He had been an infantryman in the Athenian army under Andokides, and the survivors at Megara had made their perilous escape through the hills of Boeotia back to Attica. Andokides would have told Pericles that Socrates, then twenty-four, had exhibited extraordinary strength, endurance, an utter disregard for fear, and a remarkable capacity to infuse men with those virtues. With that report, Pericles could forgive Socrates many things, including even his frequent criticism of democracy.

It is not hard to imagine some of the natural subjects of conversation between Socrates and Pericles. Socrates would probably irreverently ask Pericles if his wife was still writing his speeches. The philosopher is known to have said that Aspasia helped Pericles prepare his speeches, and Socrates was in a position to know. Pericles would probably admit it, for no one loved and respected a woman more than Pericles did Aspasia. Socrates would wonder why a man inheriting Anaxagoras' agnosticism would devote so much effort and money to the construction of a temple to a goddess. Pericles could tell him that one did not have to believe literally in a goddess to build a temple to her. If one believes in wisdom and accepts Athena as its symbol, then one may build a temple to wisdom and call it a temple to Athena. The people will still look on it as a temple to Athena, but the more Athena, in their minds, becomes the goddess of wisdom and less the goddess of war, the more wise and less warlike the people become. The leaders change the gods and the gods change the people. Socrates would understand, perhaps even advocate, such a philosophy.

They talked about democracy. Socrates would repeat what he said many times in his life that he did not support monarchy or oligarchy, nor did he entirely approve of democracy. On this occasion he would, no doubt, express to Pericles a criticism that is attributed to him by Xenophon:

> It is foolish for the rulers of the city to be established in office by lot, when nobody would want to use a pilot chosen by lot or a builder or a flutist or anyone for any other task of the sort, although far less harm is caused when mistakes are made in them than when they are made concerning the city.[65]

---

[65]Xenophon, *Memorabilia*, trans. Amy L. Bonnette (Ithaca, NY: Cornell University Press, 1994), 7, at *Mem.*, I, ii, 9.

Already we can see the genesis of Plato's *Republic* in the candid words of his teacher. Pericles could not foresee that the barefoot, shabbily dressed, whimsical young man would be revered twenty-five hundred years later as the father of philosophy. That his gadfly guest and a young man from Nazareth, to be born 438 years later, would probably influence the Western half of the world more than any other who would live in the two and a half millennia to follow.

Ictinus and Callicrates, the architects of the Parthenon, would bring their wives to the reception. At Aspasia's parties, the women came. They were not the stag symposia the men were accustomed to. With Pericles' blessing and money, she had become the hostess of the century. And hetaerae, if not wives, were gaining stature. Pericles would embrace the architects and his friend Phidias with deep affection. They were the composers of an eternal symphony in stone. They had made Pericles feel immortal. Phidias would report that the statuary on the pediments and part of the metopes had been completed but that it would take another five years to do the sculpturing he contemplated for the frieze of the cella.

Polygnotus, the painter, would come to the party, for he had supervised all and personally performed much of the painting on the temple. Polygnotus was a genius with the brush. Though he was a native of the Greek island of Thasos and not an Athenian citizen, Pericles had the assembly support him so that he could spend all his time painting for the city. Already a street in Athens had been named after him. It still bears his name.

Hippodamus, the architect and the world's first city planner, would come up from Piraeus. His miraculous remodeling of the port city, almost completed, was a source of great pride to Pericles. The functional new buildings, the wide, right-angled streets, the parks, the concentration of manufacturing in one area, commercial enterprise in another, and separating the residential sections from the clang of the armorer's hammer and the shipbuilder's saw, were the talk of the Hellas. Piraeus was the door to Attica, and everyone who had entered it en route to the Panathenaea had exulted about the magic change. Piraeus' population fecundity had begun to make it look like the garbage dump of the world. It had more than doubled in population since Hippodamus had started work on it, and his planning had redressed the old and organized the new in a fashion such as to turn the urban eyesore into a vista of beauty that had excited the envy of city rulers all over the world.

Pericles had sent Hippodamus with Herodotus and the others to Italy for a time to plan the new colonial city of Thuria. His ideas had become as international in demand as the words of Sophocles, the chisel of Phidias, the paintings of Polygnotus, or the laws of Solon.

Sophocles, of course, would be there, gregarious and garrulous as usual. It is not unlikely that Pericles selected him to supervise the entire panathenaic celebration, for the general would want it to be the most memorable show in the history of Athens, and Sophocles was the best director available. As a hostess, Aspasia would have to watch the thirty-one-year-old Socrates and the fifty-seven-year-old Sophocles to avoid a possibly unpleasant argument. Socrates would immediately try to back the playwright into a corner and cut him up with one of his cross-examinations, which were already drawing crowds at the agora. Socrates would repeat his announcement that he would never attend a play by Sophocles. He thought the only playwright whose plays were worth attending were those of Euripides. Sophocles' play, *Antigone*, written five years before, was the most popular play in Greece. His *Oedipus Rex* was yet to come. Sophocles, the favorite of the Muses, the toast of the town, had made peace with the gods. He had become preoccupied with upholding Homer's ancient deities and, in Socrates' mind, he did not write to impart knowledge which was the basis of all happiness; he wrote rather to entertain and to encourage subservience to the gods. Euripides wrote to impart knowledge and to undermine the gods and the hold they had on the people. Sophocles, according to Socrates, wrote what the people wanted to hear. Euripides wrote the truth.

Euripides would come late and alone. He resented leaving his work. Most of the guests except Socrates would bore him, for they represented the establishment that he would destroy and rebuild from new plans and specifications. He had little time or disposition to attend social functions. He would prefer to hide out in his usual working habitat, a cave on the island of Salamis, where he wrote many of his plays. He was even more of a rebel than Socrates, and while he considered Pericles somewhat conservative, he supported him because Pericles preserved freedom of expression.[66] Euripides was forty-two and impatient to replace Sophocles as Athens' premier playwright. He had not reached his zenith, for his greatest plays (*Medea*, *Electra*, and the *Trojan Women*) were yet to be written.

He did not suspect that in the twentieth century A.D. that these three plays would be performed over and over again in theatres all over the Western world year after year and made into motion pictures along with Sophocles' *Antigone* and *Oedipus Rex*. Little did either of the playwrights dream that the style and content of their plays would be copied by men with names such as Eugene O'Neill, Tennessee Williams, Arthur Miller, and Edward Albee; that their words held the same type of immortality that was built into the Parthenon. Tonight they were merely rivals seeking to cultivate and capture the minds of the men and women of

---

[66]In the Periclean society, Sophocles could praise the gods while Euripides castigated them, and they could both stay out of jail. No other such society existed between Adam and the Renaissance.

Greece.

Even their brilliant hostess, Aspasia, would not foresee that her two guests and the twelve-year-old Aristophanes would be the last good playwrights the world would know until William Shakespeare and Christopher Marlowe appeared two thousand years later.

Certainly, Pericles would send an invitation to Herodotus in far off Thuria and he would come if he possibly could, though traveling by sea from Italy was a long and sometimes treacherous journey. If he came, the guests would gather around him and hear the fascinating tales from the master storyteller about the wondrous world of the West. At forty-nine, he had seen more of the world than any of them, and the storyteller's twinkle was still in his eyes. Herodotus' most enraptured listener would be another guest—the young, high-born student of Herodotus, the twenty-five-year-old Thucydides, who at sixteen had stood in the agora, listened to Herodotus read his history and thrilled at the accounts until tears came to his eyes.

Thucydides' talent as a writer and remarkable capacity to assemble and coldly analyze facts might have motivated Pericles to hire him as an aide in spite of the fact that he was related to the obnoxious Thucydides whom Pericles had ostracized. He was probably a quiet, unsmiling youth of slim stature and medium height with alert eyes that saw everything, sharp ears that heard all, an even temper, and an aloof detachment, strange for so young a man, which enabled him to appraise men and events with unemotional objectivity. His family owned extensive gold holdings in Thrace. Because he was rich, dedicated to learning, and consumed with an interest in government and military leaders, Pericles would have spotted him and put him to work for the city at any early age. His admiration for Pericles, revealed in the history he wrote a few years later, argues that he was close to the general and deeply involved in his activities. Pericles would not realize on this night of nights that this young man's writing would some day contribute more to insure his immortality than the marble masterpiece he had dedicated that day.

Pericles, being the consummate politician he was, would not overlook the young voters. There was probably present a man younger than Thucydides, a brilliant student of medicine named Hippocrates from the island of Cos, now studying in Athens to be a physician. He was only twenty-two; about eight years later he would write an oath that today hangs on the walls of most doctors' offices in the Western world. He was a scientist who would disturb his contemporaries by writing that the gods had nothing to do with disease and illness—there were natural, discoverable causes of all maladies.

Returning from Magna Gracia with Herodotus would be another distinguished intellectual of frightening proportions, the teacher, philosopher, and super-Sophist named Protagoras. He had taught in Athens for several years then left to help found the city of Thuria on what is now the Adriatic coast of Italy. He had grown up in the city of Abdera in northern Greece where his teachings were much too advanced for consumption by his fellow townsmen. He migrated to Athens about 450 B.C. to be in the only city in the world where, it was claimed, men enjoyed freedom of speech. But he even disturbed many in that liberal city when he started some of his lectures by saying: "As to whether or not the gods really exist, I do not know." Such agnostic temerity appealed to Pericles for his teacher, Anaxagoras, had not believed in the gods. And it would appeal to many of his guests, except Sophocles, whose plots rested on the reality and omniscience of the gods, as well as the comparative frailty of man. To Sophocles, Protagoras was a dangerous man.

Pericles and Aspasia lived dangerously for people wedded to politics. In their home and in their city, variety of thought and expression was encouraged. Protagoras had coined an aphorism that formed the predominant philosophical theme of the golden age: "Man is the measure of all things."[67] He repeated the maxim over and over again in one way or another in Pericles' courtyard that happy mid-summer evening.

Pericles may have neglected his other guests for a time to talk with Protagoras for they had discussed theories of law before at length and they were both enthralled with rhetoric. Protagoras is known as the father of grammar. He taught about sentences, periods, commas, paragraphs, verbs, and their agreement. After his time, scrolls bore the marks of his mechanical revolution in the structure of rhetoric. Pericles would compliment him on his mastery of words and Protagoras would have the grace to say: "General, you create words—such as 'democracy'—and give them meaning. I merely classify them as parts of speech and line them up in disciplined squadrons so they will march in orderly fashion at your command to achieve your objectives." But Pericles knew Protagoras was more than a mechanic. He was a creator, not only of individual words and precisely structured sentences, but of challenging and revolutionary ideas.

Doubtless young Socrates and Protagoras entertained the guests part of the evening with one of their stimulating conversational combats, such as Plato later recorded, in which they took turns firing questions at each other and topping and retopping each other with brilliant answers. Protagoras was one man who could stand up to the clever Socrates in such engagements. Socrates was delighted to find among the hordes of frauds he questioned day after day a man who could think as he thought, match his logic, burrow to the crux of a question, reduce abstractions to precise definitions,

---

[67]Diogenes Laertius, *Protagoras*, Book ix, Section 51.

and express them artfully.

It would fascinate Aspasia, the mistress of rhetoric, to watch the two men and compare them—so dissimilar in their appearance and personal habits yet so similar in their intellectual capacities. She would never forget the picturesque portrait of the beautiful-ugly young man standing there in his worn, frayed tunic, and bare feet, challenging the handsome older professor who wore the most expensive linen tunic and himation and polished belt and jeweled sandals. Why? Because there was some difference of dedication and values in the two men. Socrates charged his pupils nothing, while Protagoras, the most expensive tutor in all of Greece—and worth every drachma of it, had made a fortune. But the two men glowed when they got together. Each left his mark on mankind.

With Protagoras would come a fellow Thracian from Abdera named Democritus, who also had traveled to Athens to breathe its air of freedom and teach his own esoteric and revolutionary doctrines. Some of the guests would listen for a few moments while this scientist-philosopher told them that all matter was made up of infinitesimal particles called atoms. The atom was the basic building block of everything that was animate or inanimate. When some frowned a lack of understanding, he would switch to philosophy and question the chauvinistic devotion to a polis and say: "To a wise man, the whole earth is open; for the native land of a good soul is the whole earth."[68]

At that point Pericles, who had had a love affair with Athens for at least thirty years, would hand him another drink and change the subject. It is an ironic coincidence that one of the first voices raised for the brotherhood of man laid the groundwork for the invention of the atomic bomb.

Pericles' guest list that night was indeed distinguished

---

[68]Democritus, *Ethica*, fragment 168.

—more so than he knew. Gathered in his courtyard sipping wine, eating lamb, and engaging in their favorite sport of conversation were the father of philosophy, the father of history, the father of medicine, the founder of modern architecture, the innovator of realistic painting, the two greatest playwrights to live (before William Shakespeare), the greatest sculptor to wield a chisel (before Michelangelo), the first city planner, the architect of modern rhetoric, and the originator of atomic science. All were being entertained by the first statesman to make democracy work.

And hostessing the affair and probably the most exciting personality of them all was one liberated woman, Aspasia, who proved twenty-five hundred years ago that a woman's mind can match a man's any day of the week. The fascinating discovery is that all of these remarkable men and women were contemporaries. When Pericles and Aspasia dispatched the guests at their door late that night, they said good night to most of the founders of Western civilization. It is the echo of those resonant voices that can still be heard today.

IDENTIFICATION OF MAJOR CHARACTERS

Aeschylus ('es-kə-ləs), 525-456 B.C., Greek dramatist
Anaxagoras (ˌa-ˌnak-'sa-gə-rəs), ca. 500-428 B.C., Greek philosopher
Aristophanes (ˌar-ə-'stä-fə-ˌnēz), ca. 450-ca. 388 B.C., Athenian dramatist
Aspasia (as-'pā-zhē-ə), 470?-410 B.C., consort of Pericles
Callicrates (kə-'lik-rə-ˌtēz), 5th cent. B.C., Greek architect
Cleisthenes ('klīs-thə-ˌnēz), ca. 570-after 508 B.C., Athenian statesman
Cratinus (krə--'tī-nus), ca. 484-ca.419 B.C., Athenian playwright and comic poet
Democritus (di-'mä-krə-təs), ca. 460-ca. 370 B.C., Greek philosopher
Euripides (yu-'ri-pə-ˌdēz), ca. 484-406 B.C., Greek dramatist
Heraclitus (ˌher-ə-'klī-təs), ca. 540-480 B.C., Greek philosopher
Hermippus (her-'mi-pus), fl. end of 5th cent. B.C., Greek playwright and satirical poet.
Herodotus (hi-'rä-də-təs), ca. 484-between 430 and 420 B.C., Greek historian
Hippocrates (hi-'pä-krə-ˌtēz), ca. 460-ca. 377 B.C., Greek physician
Hippodamus (hi-'pod-ə-mus), ca. 480-ca. 408 B.C., a Melesian architect, engineer, and city planner.
Ictinus (ik-'tī-nəs), 5th cent. B.C., Greek architect

Miltiades (mil-ˈtī-ə-ˌdēz), ca. 554-489? B.C., Athenian general

Myron (ˈmī-rən), fl. ca. 480-440 B.C., Greek sculptor

Pericles (ˈper-ə-ˌklēz), 490-429 B.C., Athenian statesman

Phidias (ˈfi-dē-əs), fl. ca. 490-430 B.C., Greek sculptor

Plato (ˈplā-ˌtō), ca. 428-348 B.C., Greek philosopher

Polygnotus (ˌpä-lig-ˈnō-təs), ca. 500-ca. 440 B.C., Rhodian sculptor

Praxiteles (prak-ˈsi-tᵊl-ˌēz), fl. 370-330 B.C., Athenian sculptor

Protagoras (prō-ˈta-gə-rəs), ca. 485-410 B.C., Greek philosopher

Socrates (ˈsä-krə-ˌtēz), ca. 470-399 B.C., Greek philosopher

Sophocles (ˈsä-fə-ˌklēz), ca. 496-406 B.C. , Greek dramatist

Thales (ˈthā-ˌlēz), ca. 625?-547? B.C., Greek philosopher

Thucydides (thü-ˈsi-də-ˌdēz), son of Alorus, ca. 460-401 B.C., Greek historian

Thucydides (thü-ˈsi-də-ˌdēz), son of Melesias, mid-5th cent. B.C., Athenian general and politician

Xenophon (ˈze-nə-fən), ca. 431-ca. 352 B.C., Greek historian

CHRONOLOGY OF ANCIENT GREECE[69]

By 1000 B.C.	Occupation of the Cycladic islands and the Asiatic coast by Hellenes from the European mainland
ca. 800	Homer's epic poems, the *Iliad* and the *Odyssey*, being composed
776	The first Olympic Games are held
750-700	Invention and diffusion of Greek alphabet
750-550	Age of colonization (Mediterranean and Euxine)
ca. 705	Greek architects begin building in stone
ca. 700	The poet Hesiod flourishes
	Human figures appear as main subjects in pottery painting
683-682	An aristocratic republic, ruled by archons elected for one-year terms, is established in Athens
ca. 675	The poet Archilochus flourishes in Paros
ca. 650	Large free-standing sculpture is evolved
ca. 630	The poet Alcman flourishes in Sparta
621	Draco issues the first Athenian lawcode
610-525	Attic black-figured pottery is developed
ca. 600	Athenian colony at Sigeum
	The poet Sappho flourishes in Lesbos
	The poet Alcaeus flourishes in Lesbos

---

[69]Most dates in Greek history before 500 B.C. are only approximate.

595	Earliest Greek coins minted by Aegina
594-593	Solon is archon of Athens and initiates social and constitutional reform
585	Thales of Miletus predicts eclipse of the sun
582-573	Establishment of international games circuit: Pythia (582), Isthmia (581), and Nemea (573)
ca. 580	The philosopher Anaximander flourishes
566	Reorganization of Panathenaic festival
561	Peisistratus' first tyranny at Athens
ca. 560	Athenian colonists in the Thracian Chersonese
560-546	Reign of Croesus, king of Lydia
559-556	Miltiades the Elder becomes tyrant in Thracian Chersonese
550	Control of Asiatic Hellenes by Croesus
ca. 550	Doric architecture is standardized.
	Ionic influences appear in the architecture of mainland Greece and the West
ca. 540	The poet Theognis flourishes in Megara
549-529	Reign of Cyrus the Great of Persia
548	Temple of Apollo at Delphi burned
546	Fall of Croesus to Cyrus; submission of Asiatic Hellenes
546-527	Final tyranny of Peisistratus at Athens
ca. 534	Thespis, the reputed founder of Greek tragedy, is the fist victor at Athens' drama festival
ca. 530	Attic red-figured pottery is developed
	The philosopher and mathematician Pythagoras establishes a religious fraternity at Croton
	The philosopher Xenophanes flourishes
530-450	Late Attic black-figured pottery
528-510	Peisistratus is succeeded by his sons, Hippias and Hipparchus
ca. 520	Athenian colonists on Lemnos and Imbros
	The poet Simonides of Ceos fluorishes
518	Birth of the poet Pindar

514	Darius' Scythian expedition; Persian forces in Thrace
	Hipparchus is murdered
511-510	Expulsion of Hippias
510	Fall of the Tyrants
508	Emergence of Cleisthenes; hostility of Spartans and Persians aroused by the Athenians
508-501	Adoption of Cleisthenes' constitution
506	Athenian cleruchy at Chalcis (Euboea)
501-500	Institution of Ten Generals at Athens
ca. 500	The historian Hecataeus flourishes in Miletus
	The philosopher Heraclitus teaches at Ephesus in Asia Minor
499	Beginning of Ionian Revolt from Persia
498	Athenian withdrawal
494	Fall of Miletus; end of Revolt
493-492	Themistocles, elected archon at Athens, starts fortifying the harbor of Piraeus
	Phrynichos prosecuted for play *Sack of Miletus*
492	Return of Miltiades to Athens and prosecution for tyranny
490	Darius of Persia launches an attack on mainland Greece, starting the Persian Wars. The Persians are repelled by the Athenian victory at Battle of Marathon
ca. 490	The philosopher Parmenides flourishes at Elea
	Birth of Pericles
	Birth of Herodotus
487	Ostracism used at Athens for the first time
487-486	Athenian archons chosen by lot
486	Accession of Xerxes of Persia
484	Aeschylus wins his first victory at Athens' drama festival
483	Discovery of new silver vein at Mt. Laurium
	Construction of two hundred ships at Athens

481	Meeting of "The Hellenes," under Sparta's leadership, to discuss the threat of invasion
480	The Greeks are crushed at the Battle of Thermopylae, then win a victory at Salamis
	The Acropolis is destroyed by the Persians
480-445	The sculptor Myron is at work in Athens
479	The last major battle of the war, Plataea and Mycale, end in defeat for Persia
479-478	Rebuilding of Athenian walls
478	Hellenic naval offensive
	Disgrace of Pausanias; withdrawal of Lacedaemonians
478-477	Acceptance of hegemony by the Athenians
	Organization of Delian League of Greek states against Persia
476-475	Capture of Eion and Skyros
476	Pindar's first *Olympian* ode
473	Ostracism of Themistocles
ca. 473	Carystus forced into the Delian League
472	Death of Pausanias
	Production of Aeschylus' *Persians*
471	Exile of Themistocles
470	Revolt and reduction of Naxos
469	Delian League victory at the Eurymedon
	Birth of the philosopher Socrates
468	The dramatist Sophocles introduces the use of more than two actors in tragedy
467	Production of Aeschylus' *Seven against Thebes*
465	Thasos revolts from Delian League and forced back
	Accession of Artaxerxes of Persia
465-464	Athenian defeat by Thracians at Drabescus; failure of colony at Ennea Hodoi
	Delian League successes against Persians in Hellespontine area

	Thrasian appeal to the Spartans
464	Earthquake at Sparta; revolt of Messenians
463-462	Fall of Thasos
462	Dismissal of Athenian assistance by Lecedaemonians
	The philosopher Anaxagoras comes to Athens
462-461	Athenian alliances with Argives and Thessalians
	Pericles, with the statesman Ephialtes, brings democratic reforms to Athens
461	Ostracism of Cimon from Athens
	Radical reforms of Ephialtes at Athens
	Fall of Messenian Ithome
	Settlement of Messenians at Naupactus by the Athenians
461-460	Athenian alliance with Megarians
	Revolt of Egypt (under Inaros) from Persia
461-446	War between Athens and Sparta (First Peloponnesian War)
460	Delian League expedition to Cyprus; acceptance of invitation to aid Inaros
460-454	Delain League expedition in Egypt
460	Naval engagements off the Argolid
	Athenian capture of Troezen
	Siege of Aegina
460-459	Long Walls begun to Piraeus and Phalerum
458	Spartan invasion of central Hellas
	Spartan victory at Tanagra
	Athenian victory at Oenophyta; alliances with Boeotians, Phocians, and Locrians
	Production of Aeschylus' *Oresteia*
458-457	Completion of Long Walls to protect Athens
	Athenian alliance with Segesta
457	Surrender of Aegina
	Voyage of Tolmides round Peloponnese
456	Death of Aeschylus

ca. 456	The Temple of Zeus at Olympia is completed
455	Euripides' first tragedy is performed
454	Final defeat of Dealian League in Egypt
	Delian League treasury transferred from Delos to Athens, signaling Athenian dominance
	Voyage of Pericles round Peloponnese; subjection of Achaeans
454-453	Revolts of Erythrae and Miletus
452	Recovery of Erythrae and Miletus
451	Return of Cimon
	Five-year armistice with the Peloponnesians
	Athenian citizenship is restricted
	Pay for jurors is introduced
	Pericles organizes a Panhellenic Congress
450	Expedition to Cyprus under Cimon
	Aid sent to Amyrtaeus in Egypt
	Death of Cimon
	Cleruchies sent to Lemnos, Naxos, Andros, and Carystus
449	Peace of Callias
	Failure of Panhellenic Congress
	Transfer of five thousand talents to treasury of Athens
	Decree of Clearchus about coinage
	Inception of building program at Athens
	Sacred War: Spartan interference at Delphi
448	No tribute paid (moratorium)
	Athenian alliances with Leontini and Rhegium
447	Resumption of payment of tribute
	Ictinus and Callicrates design and begin construction of the Parthenon
	Cleruchy sent to Thracian Chersonese
	Sacred War: Athenian reprisal at Delphi
447-446	Colony sent to Colophon

446	Athenian defeat at Coroneia; Athenian loss of influence in central Greece
	Revolt of Euboea and Megara
	Peloponnesian invasion of Attica
	Reduction of Euboea; cleruchies sent to Chalcis and Eretria
	Colony sent to Brea
	Pindar writes the last of his odes still extant
446-445	The Thirty-Years' Peace is declared between Athens and Sparta
	Building of southern Long Wall to Piraeus
444	Protagoras, a Sophist, draws up laws for the new colony which was sent to Thurii
443	Ostracism of Thucydides, son of Melesias
	Colonists sent to Astacus
	Sophocles made treasurer of league
442	Special celebration of Great Panathenaea
441	Sophocles made a General
	Production of Sophocles' *Ajax* and *Antigone*
440	Revolts of Samos and Byzantium
439	Recovery of Samos and Byzantium
438	Production of Euripides' *Alcestis*
	Building of the Parthenon is completed
	Phidias' statue *Athena Parthenos* is dedicated
437	Colony sent to Amphipolis
	The Propylaea, the monumental gateway to the Acropolis, is begun
436	Colonists sent to Sinope and Amisus
435	Battle of Leucimme (Corcyraeans defeat Corinthians)
434-433	Decrees of Callias
433	Athenian-Corcyraean alliance
	Renewal of alliances with Leontini and Rhegium; alliance with Sicilian Halicyae
	Battle of Sybota

	Megarian Decree
432	Revolts of Potidaea and Chalcidians; Perdiccas of Macedon hostile
	Meetings of Peloponnesian League
	Athens excludes Megara from league ports
	Phidias completes his work on the Parthenon friezes
431	The Peloponnesian War breaks out between Sparta and Athens
	Theban attack on Plataea
	Aeginetans expelled; island colonized
	Euripides' tragedy *Medea* is produced
430	Onset of the plague
	Defection in Colophon
ca. 430	Production of Sophocles' *Oedipus Tyrannus*
	The physician Hippocrates flourishes in Cos
430-429	Fall of Potidaea
429	Death of Pericles
428	Revolt of Mytilene
427	Recapture of Mytilene; debate at Athens
	Fall of Plataea to Thebans and Peloponnesians
	Sophist Gorgias of Leontini on embassy to Athens
	Athenian assistance sent to Leontini
	Renewal of alliance with Segesta
426	Recurrence of the plague
425	Peloponnesian invasion of Attica
	Athenian victory at Pylos
	Production of Aristophanes' *Acharnians*
425-424	Accession of Darius II
424	Athenian withdrawal from Sicily
	Athenian capture of Cythera
	Thucydides, the historian, is appointed an Athenian General and then exiled from Athens for his failure as a General

424-423	Athenian defeat at Delium
	Capture of Amphipolis by Brasidas
423	War is interrupted by a one-year armistice
	Brasidas' successes in Thrace
	Production of Aristophanes' *Clouds*
422	Failure and death of Cleon at Amphipolis
421	Peace of Nicias
	Reduction and punishment of Scione
	Athenian-Spartan alliance
420	Quadruple alliance (Athenians, Eleians, Mantineians, and Argives)
420-417	Intrigues of Alcibiades in the Peloponnese
419	Athens renews the war
418	Athens is defeated at the Battle of Mantineia
418-417	Spartan-Argive alliance
416	Athenian-Argive alliance
	Ostracism of Hyperbolus
	Capture of Melos by the Athenians
416-415	Expedition to Sicily voted
415	Sacrilege of the herms
	Departure of the Athenian fleet for Sicily
	Recall of Alcibiades; his flight to Sparta
	Euripides' *Trojan Women* is staged
414	Arrival of Gylippus in Sicily
	Aristophanes' comedy *The Birds* is produced
413	Occupation of Deceleia by Peloponnesians
	Replacement of tribute by five percent tax
	The naval battle at Syracuse ends in the defeat of Athens
	Euripides' *Electra* is presented
412	Alcibiades in the eastern Aegaean
	Widespread revolt in the east
	Persian intervention
411	Oligarchic revolution, restoration of democracy at Athens

	Revolt of Euboea
	Production of Aristophanes' *Lysistrata*
410	Restoration of democracy at Athens
	Tribute restored
409-406	The Erectheum is completed on the Acropolis
407	Return of Alcibiades to Athens
406	Athenian defeat at Notium
	Flight of Alcibiades
	Athenian victory at Battle of Arginusae
	Death of Sophocles
	Death of Euripides
405	The Athenian fleet is destroyed at Aegospotami in Thrace
	Siege of Athens
	Aristophanes' *The Frogs* is presented
404	Athens surrenders to Sparta
401	Posthumous production of Sophocles' *Oedipus at Colonus*
	The historian Xenophon conducts the retreat from Cunaxa
399	Socrates, tried and condemned to death, dies by drinking hemlock

BIBLIOGRAPHY

Aeschylus. *Aeschylus Plays: One*. Introduction by J. Michael Walton; trans. Frederic Raphael and Kenneth McLeish. London: Methuen Drama, 1991.

Archibald, Zofia. *Discovering the World of Ancient Greece*. New York: Facts on File, 1991.

Biers, William R. *The Archaeology of Greece: An Introduction*. Ithaca, NY: Cornell University Press, 1987.

Casson, Lionel. *The Ancient Mariners*. 2d ed. Princeton, NJ: Princeton University Press, 1991.

Crow, John A. *Greece: The Magic Spring*. New York: Harper and Row, 1970.

Henry, Madeleine M. *Prisoner of History: Aspasia of Miletus and Her Biographical Tradition*. New York: Oxford University Press, 1995.

Herodotus. *The Histories*. Trans. Aubrey de Selincourt; rev. John Marincola. London: Penguin Books, 1996.

Jenkins, Ian. *The Parthenon Frieze*. Austin: University of Texas Press, 1996.

Kagan, Donald. *Pericles of Athens and the Birth of Democracy*. New York: Free Press, 1991.

Lawrence, Arnold W. *Greek Architecture*. 5th ed. Rev. Richard A. Tomlinson. New Haven: Yale University Press, 1996.

Martin, Thomas R. *Ancient Greece*. New Haven, CT: Yale University Press, 1996.

Plutarch. *The Lives of the Noble Grecians and Romans*. Trans. John Dryden; rev. Arthur H. Clough. New York: Modern Library, 1979.

Sacks, David. *Encyclopedia of the Ancient Greek World*. New York: Facts on File, 1995.

Samuel, Alan E. *The Greeks in History*. Toronto: Edgar Kent, 1992.

Sophocles. Trans. David Grene. 2d ed. Chicago: University of Chicago Press, 1991.

Speake, Graham, ed. *A Dictionary of Ancient History*. Oxford: Basil Blackwell, 1994.

Spivey, Nigel. *Understanding Greek Sculpture: Ancient Meanings, Modern Readings*. New York: Thames and Hudson, 1996.

Stockton, David. *The Classical Athenian Democracy*. Oxford: Oxford University Press, 1990.

Thucydides. *The Landmark Thucydides: A Comprehensive Guide to the Peloponnesian War*. Ed. Robert B. Strassler; introduction by Victor D. Hanson. New York: Free Press, 1996.

Tournikiotis, Panayotis, ed. *The Parthenon and Its Impact in Modern Times*. Athens, Greece: Melissa Publishing House, 1994.

Toynbee, Arnold. *The Greeks and Their Heritages*. Oxford: Oxford University Press, 1985.

Vernant, Jean-Pierre. *The Greeks*. Trans. Charles Lambert and Teresa Lavender Fagan. Chicago: University of Chicago Press, 1995.

Xenophon. *A History of My Times (Hellenica)*. Trans. Rex Warner. Harmondsworth, England: Penguin, 1981.

_____. *Memorabilia*. Trans. Amy L. Bonnette. Ithaca, NY: Cornell University Press, 1994.

Wycherley, R. E. *The Stones of Athens*. Princeton, NJ: Princeton University Press, 1978.

INDEX OF NAMES

I

J

L

M

N

O

P

ABOUT THE AUTHORS

MARVIN J. BERTOCH (1915-1978) received a B.A. in Political Science in 1938 and an LL.B. in Law in 1941, both from the University of Utah. He was admitted to the Utah State Bar and began his professional life as a special agent for the FBI. As a practicing attorney, Marvin became a senior partner in the Ray, Quinney, and Nebeker law firm.

Marvin was a distinguished visiting scholar in Ancient Greek History at Westminster College, for which he wrote and narrated a television documentary tour of England and Greece.

Marvin received first prize in the literary awards from the Utah Institute of Fine Arts for a play. He wrote *The Little Ships*, which described his experiences as an officer aboard the LCS-121 in the Pacific during World War II. He published articles in *Mankind*, *The American Bar Association Journal*, *The American Legion Magazine*, *The International Society of Barristers Quarterly*, and *The University of Utah Alumni Magazine*.

JULIA BRIXEN BERTOCH received a B.S. in English and Speech from the University of Utah, and she was a member of Phi Kappa Phi and Beehive. In 1970 she received an M.S. degree in Speech, also from the University of Utah. During her professional life she taught English as well as Speech and Theatre in the Granite and Salt Lake School Districts and at Westminster College in Salt Lake City. Julia has served both in the National Assistance League and Operation Conquest, and she organized and was the first president of the University of Utah PMT Theatre Guild. She has been active in the Alumni Board, Chi Omega, the Emeritus Board, the Long Term Care Gerontology Center, and the Friends of the Marriott Library. In 1987 she was given the Merit of Honor Award by the University of Utah Alumni Association.

Typos

xiii

95

25 96 108

38 154 119

43

Bolbe
Olynthus
Potidaea
Mende
Sin. Thermaicus
Olympus M.
Haliacmon
Atintanes
THESSALIA
Gyrton
Larissa
Peneus Fl.
Pindus
Pharsalus
Pherae
Sinus Pagasaeus
Sciathos
Sepias Pr.
Artemisium
Thesprotia
Chemerium Pr.
Ambracia
Argos Amphilochicum
Leucas
Stratus
Thermopylae
Oeta M.
Histiaea
AETOLIA
DORIS
LOCRIS
Parnassus
Delphi
Chaeronea
BOEOTIA
Tanagra
Thebae
Ithaca
Oeniadae
Rhium Pr.
Cephallenia
Patrae
Aegium
Sin. Corinthiacus
Plataea
Eleusis
Oenoe
Dyme
ACHAEA
Cyllene
Megara
Sicyon
Corinth
Salamis
Zacynthus
Phlius
Aegina
Olympia
Heraea
ARCADIA
ARGOLIS
Mycenae
Epidaurus
Argos
Mantinea
Tiryns
Troezen
Hermione
Lepreum
PELOPONNESUS
Thyrea
Argolicus Sin.
Ithome
MESSENIA
Prasiae
Pylus
SPARTA
LACONICA
Methone
Gytheum
Sin. Messeniacus
Sin. Laconicus
Malea Pr.
Taenarus Pr.
Cythera
Mare Ionium